The Politics of Philosophy

K

The Politics of Philosophy

A Commentary on Aristotle's *Politics*

Michael Davis

Rowman & Littlefield Publishers, Inc.

, INC.

Published in the United States of America
by Rowman & Littlefield Publishers, Inc.
4720 Boston Way, Lanham, Maryland 20706

3 Henrietta Street
London, WC2E 8LU, England

British Cataloging in Publication Information Available

Library of Congress Cataloging-in-Publication Data

Davis, Michael, 1947–
The Politics of philosophy : a commentary on Aristotle's Politics
/ Michael Davis.
p.   cm.
Includes bibliographical references and index.
1. Aristotle. Politics. 2. Aristotle—Contributions in political
science. I. Aristotle. Politics. II. Title
JC71.A7D35 1996   320'.01'1–dc20   95-48150   CIP

ISBN 0–8476–8205–6 (cloth : alk. paper)
ISBN 0–8476–8206–4 (pbk.: alk. paper)

Printed in the United States of America

For Susan Heldt Davis

"I am coming," I said, "to what we likened in advance to the greatest wave. Well, it shall be said even if, just like a roaring wave, it's simply about to deluge us in laughter and ill repute."

Plato, *Republic* 473c

Contents

Preface

This book has two origins. I had been thinking about the *Politics* as a political book for many years when, in 1984, I was invited to give a talk about revolution at the Center for International Studies at Emory University. I spoke on *Politics* Book 5. Since then, the other books have fallen into place for me—not always easily or in order and usually connected to an invitation (too confidently accepted, later regretted, and, finally, much appreciated) to give a talk somewhere. For these invitations I wish to thank Harvey Mansfield, Jennifer Roberts, Bradd Shore, and the graduate student associations at Catholic University and Tulane University. That it is possible to treat the pieces of the *Politics* this way—each as an independent whole—reveals a great deal about the sort of whole the book is and describes. Perhaps I would have understood this even had practical matters not seduced me into thinking about the *Politics* one book at a time, but perhaps not.

The second origin was my study of Aristotle's *Poetics*, which taught me to see that the *Politics* as a whole, while obviously a profoundly political book, is also something else. Indeed, perhaps it is so profound because it is something else. In *The Poetry of Philosophy* I argued that if we are to be defined as both the rational and the mimetic animals, then *logos* and *mimêsis* have to be in some way one. Yet Aristotle also defines us as political animals (*Politics* 1293a7–9). Must there not then be an equally intimate relation between our rational and political natures? On the one hand, this intimacy is much more openly asserted by Aristotle than is the connection between *logos* and *mimêsis* (e.g., at *Politics* 1293a10–18). On the other hand, it is deeply puzzling. Aristotle calls politics the architectonic science (*Nicomachean Ethics* 1094a27–28) because it provides the ends for all the other sciences, and he calls metaphysics or first philosophy the ruling science and the most sovereign

(*Metaphysics* 982b5–6) for much the same reason, but, at least on the surface, politics and first philosophy do not seem to have much to do with one another. I undertook this book, in part, to think through the possibility that the connection between politics and philosophy is much deeper than is ordinarily understood and that, for Aristotle, to understand either requires the other.

For valuable discussions about the *Politics* in general and specific suggestions for improving the whole or parts of this book, I am grateful to Seth Benardete, Robert Berman, Ronna Burger, Susan Davis, Mary Nichols, Stephen Salkever, Richard Velkley, and Catherine Zuckert. My daughter, Jessica Davis, was of great help in preparing the manuscript. Once again, the Earhart Foundation has generously supported my work with several grants. A grant from the National Endowment for the Humanities assisted me in the preparation of chapter two. Chapters one, five, and seven and eight appeared in different forms as articles in *Mêtis*, *The Graduate Faculty Philosophy Journal* of the New School for Social Research, and *Interpretation*, respectively.

Introduction:
Rational Animal/Political Animal

One cannot help bringing expectations to Aristotle's *Politics*, many of which are unfavorable, not to say hostile. How can someone immersed in the problems of Athens of the fourth century B.C. and of the *polis*, a form of government that can scarcely be said any longer even to exist, have much to say to us? Furthermore, Aristotle insists on making judgments about which form of political order is best. Even though we inevitably make such judgments in practice (as well as the judgments about the best ways to live on which they are based), we are theoretically ill at ease with them. And even if in principle at ease with them, we would almost certainly disagree violently with particular features of Aristotle's account. There is no place in contemporary political discourse for speculation about natural slavery or the natural inferiority of women to men.

Even if we are positively predisposed toward the *Politics*, our expectations are somehow negatively determined. We know that for Aristotle human beings are by nature political (1253a), but we tend to understand this claim as a denial of various modern theories of the primacy of the individual. Aristotle is taken before the fact to stand in opposition to the state-of-nature theories of Hobbes, Locke, and Rousseau, according to which political life is not natural but a product of human art. Now, if political life is a human artifact, the individual must be in some sense complete prior to society. Our need for political life is then a sign of our permanent alienation from nature. Aristotle's alternative seems to suggest that we who are by nature political can for that reason live naturally, and so, happily, within a political order. Drawn to the *Politics* with some hope, we approve of Aristotle's attempt to show how political life grows naturally, rather like a flower, out of other natural human associations. According to the first book of the *Politics*, political life ultimately originates in sex; nothing seems more natural.

1

At the same time, however, we are skeptical. This possibility of overcoming the tension between public and private seems a little coercive. We cannot help noticing that one of the "natural associations" to which Aristotle refers is natural slavery. This makes us especially uncomfortable when we see how much seems to depend on what, given Aristotle's understanding, can only be a small percentage of the population. Natural slaves are those who participate in reason to the extent of perceiving but not themselves thinking what is rational; it is, therefore, difficult to believe that they would be sufficiently numerous to be a part of the average household. Thus, making slavery a regular part of the household that grows into the *polis* inevitably calls into question the naturalness of the household, and so of the *polis*.

Accordingly, while we may be drawn to the naturalness of the origin of the *polis*, that is, sex, we cannot help remembering that *poleis* do not grow like flowers. They are instituted. And more often than not, as the paradigmatic cases of founders, Cain and Romulus, suggest, this involves violence—even fratricidal violence. Our expectations concerning the origin of politics are therefore at odds. Thinking about sex and violence leads us to wonder whether Aristotle's *Politics* is not a very problematic book. This is all to the good, since the problem we sense in approaching the book turns out to be the problem it is about. The *Politics* is an attempt to reconcile the *polis* as a product of growth with the *polis* as a product of human freedom. We both grow into political life and make it.

It is a commonplace to point to the intimate connection between the *Politics* and Aristotle's *Nicomachean Ethics*. Signs of this connection are everywhere. Aristotle begins the *Politics* (1252a4–7) by identifying the *polis* as the association concerned with the comprehensive and authoritative human good (at which all human action ultimately aims, according to *Nicomachean Ethics* 1094a1–23). He concludes in Book 8 with an account of how to educate men to be at once good citizens of the best regime and, since the goal of the best regime is to make its citizens happy, good men. The *Nicomachean Ethics* begins by identifying the science of what is best with politics (1094a27–29) and ends by making it clear that being good requires being raised nobly, which almost always means being raised under good laws (1179b30–34). Thus, if the end of the *Politics* points to the goal of politics as education to virtue, the end of the *Nicomachean Ethics* points to the necessity of the *polis* as a means to the education to virtue. All of this makes a certain sense. In the *Nicomachean Ethics* Aristotle indicates that human virtue is rooted in our natures as rational (1102a5–1103a11). Since human beings are naturally political, it should be no surprise that there is a connection between virtue (and ultimately happiness) and life in the *polis*.

The connection between virtue and politics is complicated, however, by the problematic character of virtue as Aristotle understands it. In the *Nicomachean Ethics* the problems are present at the very outset. Aristotle begins with the claim that all human action seems to aim at some good and then argues that this means that there must be a single best or highest good that is for its own sake and not for something else. The science of this authoritative good is called politics. Then, however, having argued for the necessity of a single "best," Aristotle splits the object of this science into two—the beautiful or noble things (*ta kala*) and the just things (*ta dikaia*). How, then, is the good at which all things aim one?

The first virtue Aristotle treats in the *Nicomachean Ethics* is courage (*andreia*). Virtue is supposed to be desirable for its own sake. The paradigmatic case of courage is, according to Aristotle, courage in war (1115a). But war is at best a necessary evil— "War is for the sake of peace" (*Politics* 1333a35). Courage, then, can come into being only when preceded by an evil. Moderation (*sophrôsunê*) has a similar structure. It is a virtue only in a being who is potentially immoderate. Aristotle knows about this difficulty, as is clear from his discussion of shame (*aidôs*) at the end of *Nicomachean Ethics* Book 4 (1128b10–36). Shame is not properly a virtue because it presupposes that something bad has been done for which one ought to feel ashamed. While good in a certain context, it is not simply good, for the context it presupposes is itself defective. This similarity between shame on one hand and courage and moderation on the other moves Aristotle to say that the latter "seem to be the virtues of the irrational parts" (*Nicomachean Ethics* 1117b24–25). However, when one presses the issue, it becomes clear that this is the structure of all of the moral virtues. Moral virtue can be the goal only for a being attempting to overcome imperfection. The imperfection of our condition makes possible our striving and so is good. However, it cannot be understood as good without undermining the rationale for our striving.

Aristotle speaks three times about the unity of the moral virtues in the *Nicomachean Ethics*. In Book 4 he calls pride or greatness of soul (*megalopsukhia*) an ornament (*kosmos*) of the virtues without which they are incomplete and therefore not virtues (1124a). In Book 5 he calls justice the sum of the virtues and complete or perfect virtue insofar as it is concerned with other human beings (1129b). Finally, in Book 6, Aristotle says that prudence (*phronêsis*) makes moral virtue possible and is made possible by it (1144b). In each instance the apparent unity of moral virtue is problematic, and in each case the problem is similar.

Crudely put, pride means being good and knowing it. It is the pleasure we take in our own virtue and therefore requires that we be aware of our own virtue as virtue. But how does the man proud because he is so self-sufficient and godlike that he wonders at nothing come to know that he is virtuous? Honors. But the life of honor was rejected earlier in the *Nicomachean Ethics* (1095b) as insufficiently self-sufficient. The proud man ought not to depend on others, but when he thinks of himself as worthy he can only do so by thinking of himself as worthy of honor, and that means the honor of others. Self-knowledge requires that we look at ourselves as though we were other; we must look at ourselves through the eyes of others. It seems then to be at odds with that godlike self-sufficiency that is the warrant for pride. The proud man lacks either self-sufficiency or self-knowledge; in either case, he cannot be proud, for to be proud one must know oneself to be self-sufficient.

The problem of pride points in two directions. Lack of self-sufficiency means dependency. If we can complete ourselves only through others, we are directed toward political life and its characteristic virtue—justice. However, the problem of self-knowledge points to Aristotle's account of the intellectual virtues in Book 6. According to Aristotle, justice can be the sum of the virtues because it makes it possible for us to share our lives with a view to self-sufficiency (1134a), and self-sufficiency is the core of virtue. Still, collective self-sufficiency is a constant reminder of individual dependence. Thus, although, as it is actually practiced in political life, justice is concerned with the equitable distribution of goods, the need for such a distribution indicates that there is not an inexhaustible supply of goods. Good things are scarce enough to be in demand. Like courage, justice is concerned with a harsh fact about human life.

Pride also pointed to the problem of self-knowledge. When we turn to Book 6 seeking some resolution of this difficulty, we discover a new set of ambiguities. Part of intellectual virtue is concerned with the essentially unchanging; the other part is concerned with the constantly changing. The unity of intellectual virtue would seem to require that one of the two parts predominate, but the highest element, *sophia*, or wisdom, by the very virtue of being highest, cannot predominate. It is by nature concerned with what does not change. On the other hand, that *phronêsis*, which is lower, should rule seems strange and even contrary to nature. Virtue seems to require self-knowledge. But self-knowledge requires that we turn away from what is timeless and most important and turn toward ourselves. But to do this is to forsake the highest capacity of our reason, the exercise of which is virtue. Virtue therefore requires that we forsake virtue.

The *Nicomachean Ethics* as a whole is the working out of the problematic nature of human virtue and so of human nature itself—first within the particular virtues themselves and then in the relations among the particular virtues that culminate in the tension between the godlike self-sufficiency of pride and the acknowledged mutual dependence of justice. The problem is then worked through in terms of the tension between the whole of moral virtue, understood as the correct disposition of our appetites, and intellectual virtue and appears again within intellectual virtue itself in the tension between *sophia* and *phronêsis*. Aristotle makes some attempts to unify these dualisms by way of some third thing. However, each third itself inevitably reproduces the dualism within itself. For example, friendship, which seems meant as a bridge between virtue understood as complete autonomy and the lack of autonomy manifest in every example of virtue in the *Nicomachean Ethics*, is given a double account. Roughly, Book 8 emphasizes how much we need friends, especially for self-knowledge, and Book 9 tells us that we are our own best friends.

The problematic character of human nature is rooted in Aristotle's analysis of the soul at the end of Book 1. The soul seems to divide into rational and nonrational parts. The nonrational divides into a vegetative and an appetitive part. The rational divides into a purely theoretical part and a part that issues commands, which the appetitive part can obey or not. Virtue, as the rational activity of soul, is either intellectual or moral, depending on the part of the rational soul of which it is the perfection. That things are not quite as simple as they seem begins to emerge when Aristotle tells us twice that this division between rational and nonrational might well be a division only by reason or speech (*logos*) and not a real division (1102a30–34, 1102b25–26). The distinct parts of the soul might be like the convex and the concave, differing from one another, but correlative sides of the same curve and requiring an act of thought to distinguish them. This must be understood in light of the queer fact that in Book 1 Aristotle never specifies what he means by that part of the soul that commands the appetites. The appetitive part of the soul is capable of listening to reason and in this way is said also to be rational. But when articulating the rational part of the soul, Aristotle says only that "the part having *logos* will also be double—[having *logos*] on the one hand sovereignly and in itself, and on the other like listening to a father" (1103a2–4). Now, the part compared to a child is clearly not in command; it is presumably no more praiseworthy or capable of virtue than are children (1100a1–4). This part "has reason" from an external source, as we are governed by parents or friends and not as mathematicians are governed by reason (1102b31–35). But if theoretical reason governs only itself, and practical reason means being governed by another, where does moral virtue fit in? How are the two parts of the rational animal, the rational and nonrational parts of soul, bound together?

Either the soul that seemed to divide so neatly into two is only problematically one soul, or it divides only problematically into two. Either we are rational and animal, and the two parts of us are at odds, or we are whole, but we cannot really be understood as rational animals. Aristotle makes the difficulty clear at the end of Book 7 where he says first that "nothing can give us pleasure always with respect to the same thing because our natures are not simple" and adds only a few sentences later that "just as a changeable man is base, so also is a nature needing change, for it is not simple or equitable" (1154b). Prudence in its attachment to the changing bears witness to the connection between virtue and change. Moral virtue in general, like courage in particular, presupposes "war," although its goal is peace. Accordingly, the need for moral virtue is a sign of the defect of our natures even though the goal of moral virtue is the perfection of our natures. Unlike most other beings, human beings are class jumpers. The perfect horse would still be a horse; the perfect human being would be a god.

All of this points back to Aristotle's initial distinction within the good between the beautiful and the just. The human good splits between what is understood as simply good and what is understood as human. Aristotle called justice the human virtue and said the proud man was like a god. These two, the beautiful and the just, were said to be the subject of political science. One would therefore expect the problems growing out of their separation to show up in the *Politics*. They appear in the very first sentences.

> Since we see that every *polis* is an association, and every association has been constituted for the sake of some good (for everyone does everything for the sake of what seems to be good), it is clear that all associations aim at some good, but the [association] most sovereign of all and comprehending all the rest [aims] especially at the most sovereign of all [goods]. This is what is called the *polis* and the political community. (1252a1–7)

This beginning is peculiar in several ways. While "we see" that every *polis* is an association, the purpose of this association is available to us only on the level of seeming, of *doxa*. Aristotle really begins with two *poleis*. On the one hand, the *polis* is comprehensive. As the complete community, it presumably embraces all varieties of human beings. As all are members of the community, all will be in some measure equal. They have all been admitted by virtue of their humanity. The comprehensive *polis* is at some fundamental level democratic. Its concern will be justice—the human virtue. On the other hand, the *polis* is sovereign or authoritative.[1] As such, it will involve principles of hierarchy that point to the good. Yet it is not at all clear what connects these two *poleis*. What is the connection between the *polis* understood as a collection of free men and the *polis* understood as a collection of beings ruled for their common good? We see enough at the beginning to realize that the two elements that were at odds in our preliminary expectations of the *Politics* are present here. Aristotle begins the *Politics* by reflecting on the necessity of combining two things not easily combined: freedom, and the equality it suggests, and the good, and the hierarchy it demands.[2]

The issue can be put still differently. Aristotle claims that the *polis* exists by nature. His view of nature is teleological; the *polis* has a *telos*—a natural end or purpose. But *telios*, the adjective formed from *telos*, also means perfect. If nature were perfect there would be no need for political communities. Men would not have associations that "seemed" anything to them. Associations would be like beehives. That men institute cities, that they do not grow as though from seeds, means that nature is not simply teleological. And yet neither can nature be chaotic, for in a simply chaotic world men could not form associations. The *polis* thus both denies and requires teleology—the goodness of nature. That Aristotle calls man the political animal is therefore instructive. It means that human beings are the locus in the world of what might be called incomplete teleology. Apart from the *polis*, men are either gods—they do not need political life—or they are beasts—they are incapable of political life. Beasts are mechanically governed by their passions; gods would be mechanically governed by their reason. That we are by nature political places us in the dark area between these extremes.

It is no accident that this brief sketch of the problematic character of political life should so easily remind one of the problematic character of philosophy. The political animal is the rational animal. The *polis* is at once an expression of order and disorder; without either, it ceases to be what it is. Philosophy shares this essentially double nature. It is impossible unless we live in an ordered world. Only in an ordered world could fundamental questions become manifest. At the same time, philosophy is both unnecessary and impossible if we live in a fully ordered world. Incomplete teleology is the necessary condition for both philosophy and political life.

This uncanny bond between man as rational and man as political is the thread running through the argument of Aristotle's *Politics*. It allows Aristotle to use philosophy as a paradigm for the best political order. This is not to say that the best *polis* will be constructed according to a particular philosophy. That the city needs philosophy—but not *a* philosophy—has something to do with the beginning of the *Politics*—the naturalness of the *polis*. The *polis* does not seem natural. Like the cave of *Republic* Book 7, it seems filled with artifice and reflections of artifice. We think of the wood out of which our houses are built as matter for carpentry. Seldom do we think of its grain as once having been a system of organs that sustained a tree. Civilized life transforms nature so as to make it seem only the raw material for realizing human schemes. The danger is that we will appear self-sufficient to ourselves. First we make the distinction between nature and convention; then, we understand political life to be entirely artificial or conventional. The next step is to think of human life as altogether malleable. Thinking about nature serves as a check on this tendency; we survey an ordered world in which we do not rule.

At the same time, Socrates, for one, thought that the rocks and trees had nothing to teach him.[3] The turn to nature is not sufficient unless, in reminding us of a sphere in which we do not rule, it also reminds us of the naturalness of our own conventionality. On one level, Platonic dialogues are always attempts to undermine conventional understanding—*doxa*—by an appeal to something beyond convention—nature. Conventional Platonic scholarship recognizes this. However, on a deeper level, the dialogues are attempts to give an account of the natural origins of the *doxa* they undermine. Plato is not simply interested in showing Socrates refute Thrasymachus' understanding of justice. He wants to show as well the natural origin of this mistaken understanding of justice. That political life is natural does not seem to be a Platonic theme because the first level of a dialogue always undercuts convention in the name of nature. However, the dialogue as a whole displays the natural origins of these mistaken conventions. That human beings are political by nature means that our nature is to live according to conventions— artificially. At the same time, these conventions are not creations *ex nihilo*. They emerge out of our natures. Plato is concerned to display human nature as it can only show itself in the tension between convention and nature. Accordingly, Platonic dialogues are adversarial.

In making the case that the *polis* is natural, Aristotle at first seems to disagree with his teacher. However, he too understands that for men to be political by nature does not mean that they are like trees or, for that matter, bees. That we are political means that we live according to certain standards that we establish for ourselves, *no-moi*—laws or conventions. We cannot live together without thinking about why we are living together. To be sure, we may look *to* nature for guidance about how to live together. It may even be our nature to do so. But we do not fall in with each other effortlessly or mechanically. However natural, the *polis* does not grow like a plant; it is established or set up.

Every *polis* will be governed by certain principles. The conditions that make those principles "self-evident," however, will tend to be undermined by the *polis* they establish. A *polis* might be founded on the self-evident principle that all men are created equal. The principle would be clear to the founders in contrast to the previous regime, in which some were treated as more human than others. These founders would then have been moved to reflect on the fundamental equality of all human beings as agents responsible for their own actions and lives—all sharing what it means at bottom to be a person, a self-conscious longing to be happy. But a regime founded on this fundamental equality of all men, unless it preserved an awareness of the previous regime against which it was a reaction, would tend to lose sight of the nature of the equality it celebrated. "All men are created equal" might then be taken to mean that no relevant distinctions exist among men. Thus, for example, some generations later, an extremely intelligent child might be raised so as either to deny or be embarrassed by his superior intelligence. A regime that does not preserve within itself some sense of the conditions to which it was initially the response will therefore tend to create the conditions for a new revolution. The democratic "truth" emerges as a corrective to the decayed aristocratic "truth." But democracy, once established, is equally liable to decay.

The first part of the *Politics*, Books 1–3, is a general account of the tension between what is good for the *polis* and the knowledge of what is good for the *polis*. It has as its theme the problematic status of both political philosophy and philosophical politics. Books 4–6 deal with how one regime is transformed into another because of the transformation of a truth seen in its context to a doctrine—a *doxa*, or what one might call the decay of philosophy into ideology. All political regimes are for this reason unstable. However, a regime constituted so as to contain within itself the alternative in light of which its fundamental principle makes sense will be more stable than most. If Books 4–6 are about the tension between the democratic and oligarchic elements of any city, Books 7–8 are about the attempt through institutions and education to locate tensions like the one between oligarchy and democracy within individual citizens. To say that the best political order is based on philosophy rather than on *a* philosophy, thus, means that it will not be a *polis* with an oligarchic or democratic or aristocratic ideology. No reigning dogma will utterly drive out all competitors. For if it were to do so, the question to which the dogma was an answer would cease to be asked, at which point the answer would cease to be intelligible as an answer. Political life, like philosophy, requires that the question remain in the answer if the answer is to be an answer. It therefore requires that the answer not be perceived as a perfect answer.

This means that there will be a variety of good regimes. A democracy that keeps aristocracy in mind will be different, but not so very different, from an aristocracy that keeps democracy in mind. At the same time, all of these regimes, if less flawed, will still be flawed. It is one thing artfully to allow for the continuation within the regime of the principle of the opposing regime. It is another really to reproduce the conditions of the initial founding. It would be absurd to expect a *polis* to keep itself in a state of constant revolution for the sake of its own health and stability. At best, one can hope for symbolic revolution, but even this will inevitably lead to a dogma of its own.

Part I

Philosophy and Politics

Chapter One

Cannibalism and Nature: *Politics* Book 1

The natural way of interpreting Book 1 of Aristotle's *Politics* has a great deal to be said for it. As we have seen, in accepting without question the primacy of the individual, our age commits itself to understanding political life as an artifact; we are not by nature political. Because political life is thought to be wholly conventional, whatever satisfaction we gain from it seems necessarily incomplete. It is the reminder of our permanent alienation from nature. Aristotle, more wholesome, argues that we are political by nature. Much of Book 1 is therefore concerned with linking the *polis* to what seems the most obviously natural of human associations—the household or *oikia*.

> Hence every *polis* is by nature if the first communities are [by nature]. (1252b30–31)

At the same time, Aristotle does not understand the *polis* to be simply a big family. Families are different in kind (*eidos*) from *poleis*. If, as Aristotle suggests, the origin of the family is the coupling of male and female, then families happen to us as a result of natural urges (1252a26–30). Cities, however, are instituted (1253a30). This clear difference sets the task of *Politics* 1—to give an account of the *polis* that understands it as growing from earlier natural associations while not denying that cities begin differently from households. Aristotle must reconcile the *polis* as a product of growth with the *polis* as a product of human freedom.

If the naturalness of the *polis* turns on its relation to the household, and the intent of Book 1 is to argue that the *polis* is natural, then Aristotle's procedure seems reasonable. He begins by explaining in what sense the household is natural. The household is comprised of family and slaves, that is, of those who are born into it and those who in some way become members of it (1253b4–11). Ironically, the former are free and the latter slaves. Frcc and slave are the extremes in terms of which the household must be understood. The case of wives is particularly delicate since they are neither born into the household, nor are they slaves. Because they seem to be a combination of both elements of the household, and because the rule of husbands over wives is said to be "political" (1259b1), the question of the status of wives will point to the question of the status of the household both as a whole and in its relation to the *polis*. Aristotle must show how slave and free can be combined in a natural whole. To do so, he attempts to show that each can be natural.

Since slavery is the more obviously problematic, Aristotle begins with the question of natural slavery (1253b14–1255b40). However, here things begin to get a little peculiar. Aristotle considers the relations between husband and wife and between father and children at the end of Book 1 (1259a37–b17) but very briefly and only in relation to the question of slavery. Between the two accounts of slavery is a long account of *oikonomikê*, the art of the household, and particularly an account of *khrêmatistikê*—that part of this art concerned with the acquisition of property. Now, while Aristotle says that the art of the household is much more concerned with its human members than with lifeless property (1239b18–21), it is curious that a full third of Book 1, more by far than is devoted to anything else, is concerned with property.

There is something in Book 1 no less curious, but more difficult to get at. Aristotle wishes to argue that there are such things as natural slaves, that the rule of master over slave is distinct from the rule of husband over wife and father over children, and that while the household is the original association by nature, it points beyond itself to the *polis* as its completion. In support of these claims, he introduces a series of quotations from the poets.

The barbarians, says Aristotle, do not distinguish between slaves and women. This is a sign that there are no natural rulers among them. Barbarians are strong evidence that there is such a thing as natural slavery: "And it is seemly that Greeks rule barbarians" (1252b8). The quotation is from Euripides' *Iphigeneia in Aulis* (1.1400). Iphigeneia, who is speaking, is about to be sacrificed by her father, Agamemnon, to propitiate the gods so that the Greeks can continue their expedition against Troy. Is this less barbaric than treating women as slaves? Iphigeneia is a living instrument used for the sake of an action.

Lest we think this is simply a mistake, four lines later Aristotle quotes Hesiod's *Works and Days* (1.405): "First a house and a woman and an ox for plowing. . . ." (1252b12). Aristotle stops there; however Hesiod continues: "a slave, and not a wife, who would follow the ox and make everything needful in the home" (ll.406–7). This is strange support for the view that the Greeks distinguish themselves from barbarians by understanding the difference between women and slaves.

Also strange is Aristotle's account of the fact that cities were originally ruled by kings. He points out that households, from which the first cities grew, are ordinarily ruled monarchically by the eldest. This is sensible enough, but for evidence he quotes Homer (*Odyssey* 9.114–15): "And each lays down the law to children and even spouses" (1252b24). The context is the description of the lives of the cyclopes. Aristotle cites as the prototype for monarchic rule beings known more for cannibalism than anything else.

Once again, one might think this veiled reference to cannibalism unintentional. But Aristotle does nothing in vain. He indicates very early the importance of cannibalism (and incest) for understanding human beings.

> For just as man, when perfected, is the best of the animals, when separated from law and justice he is the worst of all. . . . Hence without virtue he is the most unholy and savage and with regard to sex and food the worst. (1253a31–37)

Cannibalism returns as an issue, albeit indirectly, in Aristotle's discussion of the natural forms of acquisition. He begins (1256a19–40) by distinguishing among lives on the basis of the kinds (*eidê*) of food that men and animals eat to support their lives. The result is that human lives divide into nomadic, farming, and hunting. Hunting in turn subdivides on the basis of what is hunted, and includes the hunting of birds and land animals, fishing, and robbing. In the course of the account, Aristotle mentions that living the life of a nomad is like "farming a living farm" (1256a34–35). Herd animals are certainly understood by Aristotle to be a kind of property. And as "the cow serves instead of a servant to the poor" (1252b12), the relation of men to the earth is apparently the same as that of master to slave. The link between them is property.

But what is the connection between cannibalism and property? While in the process of making clear that the various ways of life can be mixed together, Aristotle mixes them in a peculiar manner.

> But some also live pleasantly by mixing some of these . . . such as the nomadic together with the life of robbing, the life of farming and that of hunting, and similarly also concerning the others. . . . (1256b2–6)

Thus Aristotle specifically couples the nomadic life and the life of robbing, and the farming life and the hunting life. But he had previously said that the nomadic life was equivalent to portable farming. The two groups would then be paired as follows:

> farmers of plants and hunters of animals
> farmers of animals and robbers.

While this is not an argument, the parallel is suggestive. Robbers are in a way also hunters—of men. Aristotle admits as much directly after he says that nature makes nothing in vain—and has made animals for the sake of men.

> Hence even the art of war is by nature an art of acquiring (for the art of hunting is a part of it) which one ought to use both against beasts and those human beings who by nature are meant to be ruled, but who are not willing, since this war is by nature just. (1256b23–26)

Yet hunting men for the purpose of making them natural slaves, like domesticating wild animals, seems instrumental to a sort of nomadic life. Natural slavery is more like farming men than hunting them. When understood in this way, we see that Aristotle has arranged his account to suggest, but avoid explicit mention of, the possibility of hunting men to eat them.[4] Since Aristotle admits that we hunt both for tools and for food, and that domesticated animals are raised both for their use and for food, if natural slaves are a species of property, cannibalism is the unmentioned possibility. The question, of course, is why.[5]

We now have several unresolved puzzles. Why the indirect concern for cannibalism in Book 1 of the *Politics*? Why the confusion about the roles of women and slaves? And why the emphasis on property and the acquisition of property in the account of the art of the household? Perhaps we can gain some clarity concerning these problems by introducing still another.

The central question of Book 1 is clearly the naturalness of the *polis*, but what nature means here is not altogether clear. It emerges as an issue in a double way. Male and female couple naturally out of a sense of mutual need. Nature's purpose (but not theirs) is the generation of offspring. Mutual need suggests a certain equality. Natural slavery, on the other hand, while having as its goal security, is based on the natural intellectual superiority of the ruler to the ruled. What is common or shared (*koinon*) in this community or association (*koinônia*) is much harder to make out. While the slave may be by nature suited to perform the bodily work that the master's soul prescribes, it is not at all clear in whose interest the work will be done. It would seem that the master cannot be trusted to rule justly unless no advantage comes to him from ruling. But then, why should he rule unless he has need of his slave? The principle of equality that seems implied by a community of men is elusive here.[6] The relation is much more obviously hierarchical. Nature may make nothing that, like the "Delphic knife," has a dual purpose, but this restriction seems not to apply to nature itself. We are naturally political beings, but the root of our political nature is twofold; it is both egalitarian and hierarchical. The *polis* is not only the highest or most sovereign human *koinônia*; it is also the most comprehensive (1252a1–6). It is not yet clear that the elements of this dual origin are entirely compatible.

The *polis* is natural because it is the end toward which the growth of the household into the village points. The household originates out of natural needs; the village is simply a more complex way of fulfilling these same needs. While, both point toward self-sufficiency, neither is adequate for achieving it. Since the self-sufficiency of human beings requires the good life and not simply life, the final association, the *polis*, is qualitatively different from those which came before. Only within it is happiness possible. Accordingly, human nature points toward the *polis* as its natural completion. We are political to an extent far greater than other animals because we have a class characteristic, an *eidos*, that suits us for this sort of living together. Human beings are the animals with speech, with *logos*, which Aristotle says is for the sake of making clear the useful and the harmful and the just and the unjust (1253a14–15). Although, as we have seen, there is a troubling doubleness to this account of the purpose of *logos*, still, nature is understood as what distinguishes one class of beings from another. We are the best of animals when we reach our end or perfection and the worst when utterly separated from political life. Perfection is understood as fulfilling the potential of the species. Consequently, while an hierarchical principle is certainly at work, the hierarchy is presented within a framework of relative equality. In the *polis* we are all human but outside the *polis* either beasts or gods.

It should now be somewhat clearer why the issue of natural slavery is so central to the argument of Book 1. If natural slaves are part of the household, and ultimately of the *polis*, then they must be understood as men, sharing a good in common with the other members of the community. If they cannot be understood as sharing such a good, they will have to be understood as beasts. Insofar as they are present in the *polis*, they will have the status of property. Property is something that is "simply of another" (1254a10). Aristotle makes it clear that slaves are a species of property.

> What then the nature and the power of the slave is, is clear from these things. For he who while being a man is not of himself [his own] but of another, he is by nature a slave; and he is another's man who, while being a man, is a piece of property; and a piece of property is a tool for action and separable [from its owner]. (1254a13–17)

However, men can only be understood as property when they are understood to be defective as men. Are natural slaves men if they share "in *logos* to such an extent as to perceive it, but not to have it" (1254b22–23)? It is not hard to imagine such beings; what is difficult is to call them natural given Aristotle's previous description of nature. The argument for the naturalness of the *polis* has been that it is the oak of which the household is the acorn; the *polis* is the *telos*—the goal, purpose, or end—toward which all prior associations aim and that alone fulfills their intent. But how can a natural slave, a sort of short circuiting of this teleology, be understood as natural? No wonder nature did not follow through on its "intention" and make the bodies of slaves correspond to their souls. Slaves themselves are a sign that nature has been unable to do what it "intended." Aristotle tells us that according to Theodectes' Helen her genealogy rather than her looks signals that she is not a slave (1255a36–38).

What, then, precisely does the "nature" of the natural slave consist in? Either a natural slave is a man (in which case his nature would be to be a fully mature man), or he is not a man (in which case master and slave are not of the same species). But beings of different species do not form a community, and thus, natural slavery cannot be one of the elements of that natural association, the household, which grows into the *polis*.

The question of natural slavery goes still further.

Since this is apparent, that if they [the free] should be as distinct in respect to body as are the images of the gods, all would say those falling short to be worthy of being enslaved by them. (1254b34–36)

Aristotle suggests a striking proportion. If nature had succeeded in its intention that the bodies of men reflect their souls, then the bodies of slaves would be to the bodies of the free as the bodies of men generally are to images of the gods—that is, depictions of the bodies of gods. However, natural slaves are defective men. Are the gods images of what men would be were they not defective? This suggestion is echoed elsewhere in Aristotle. Consider, for example, the following remarks from *Nicomachean Ethics* Book 7:

Nothing pleases us always in the same way on account of our nature's not being simple . . .

Hence god enjoys one simple pleasure always.

For just as the changeable man is bad, so also is the nature needing change; for it is neither simple nor good [meet]. (1154b21–32)

And again in Book 10:

But such a life [the contemplative life] would be greater than the human. For not by his being man will he live so, but by something divine being present in him. (1177b27–29)

If the perfect man—the *telos* or nature of man—is god, then to be human is to be necessarily imperfect. Human beings are the beings who in becoming perfect would jump their class and become something other than what they are.

This has enormous implications for the association devoted to the comprehensive and highest human good. Where, after all, do the gods live? Just as we tend to make the *eidê* of the gods similar to our own *eidos*, we tend to think of them as living the sorts of lives we live, and hence, for example, as governed by a king, Zeus (1252b24–26). At the same time, one who had no part in the *polis* either because he was unable or because he had no need would be either a beast or a god (1253a27–29). Gods do not live in cities. But if the nature of man, in the sense of his *telos*, is god, in what sense is man a political animal? In what sense is the city by nature? The *polis* may be the vehicle for our perfection; it is also the sign of our imperfection.

The discussion of natural slavery in Book 1, therefore, is not simply for its own sake. It is instrumental to the more important discussion of whether man is naturally political. Aristotle uses both natural slaves and gods as means to analyze the problematic character of human nature. The question with which Aristotle begins, the naturalness of the *polis*, is a way of asking another question: Is it possible to give an account of human life as good, while retaining its character as human? In what sense is it possible for a defective being to be natural?

That this is the problem may be seen in another way. Aristotle's first account of nature (1252b31–36) was teleological, but teleology was confined within natural classes. At 1256b7–22 Aristotle begins an account of another, much stronger, sort of teleology.

> Such property, then, appears to be given to all by nature itself, just as directly upon first being born, so also having matured. For even at birth, some animals bring forth with them from the beginning sufficient food until the offspring can provide for itself. . . . So it is clear that it must be supposed that similarly for those having been born, plants are for the sake of animals, and the other animals for the sake of men. . . . If then nature makes nothing without a purpose (*ateles*) or in vain, it is necessary for nature to have made all these things for the sake of men.

This is altogether different from what we saw earlier.[7] Not only do acorns have a *telos*—that is, not only is there teleology within classes—but there is now also a teleology cutting across classes; acorns are for the sake of squirrels. Everything is now ultimately understood to be for the sake of the highest class.

In one way, this is a great advance. In the immediate context Aristotle uses this strong teleology to justify the hunting of natural slaves, who can now be understood as natural in the sense that they are for the sake of their masters—those higher on the teleological ladder. The slave's good must finally be understood in terms of the good of the master. This seems to be what Aristotle means by likening slaves to parts and masters to the whole. The slave is nothing apart from the master, for the master provides the end or purpose for the slave.[8]

However, something has been lost. Natural slavery was meant to serve as an element of an association, the household, that is the seed of *the polis*. But if the *polis* is anything it is a *human* association. The strong teleology that cuts across classes seems to have been purchased at the price of the classes that it cuts across. It was needed to justify natural slavery, but in so doing it severs the species connection between natural slaves and their masters. The relationship ceases to be one between men of different ranks and becomes understandable wholly in terms of property. The slave is a tool for a use set by the being who uses him. But this relation now serves as a paradigm for all relations between lower and higher beings. What first emerged as an hierarchical principle within the whole, useful for defining the relations between classes, has now been used within a class, man, in such a way as to generate two new classes. But there is no reason to stop here. In principle, what the strong teleology means is that all lower beings are defined in terms of their use to higher beings. But classes of beings are defined in terms of their common purpose. If the only beings who can properly be said to belong to a class are those who are perfect instances of the class character of the class, then the strong teleology means the destruction of the possibility of hierarchy within a class. Finally that means the destruction of classes altogether. The defective man becomes a beast; the good man becomes a god. Also destroyed, although it seems almost anticlimactic to say so, is the possibility of a community based on a mutual good.

The *polis*, like all associations, can exist only as a mixture of hierarchy and equality. Book 1 of the *Politics* is primarily concerned with hierarchy as a principle of association and with the tragic implications of its unlimited extension.⁹ It is in this context that cannibalism, the confusion of women and slaves, and the emphasis on property become particularly important.

Cannibalism is simply the strong teleology gone wild. It is the natural result of understanding other men solely in terms of their use—as having a good only as parts of another being. A natural slave, lacking any *telos* of his own, is potentially swallowed up by his master in more than a metaphorical sense. Aristotle seems to agree with Kant that it is necessary to treat other men never simply as means, but also as "ends in themselves." To deny that human beings are in part ends in themselves is to deny that they are human. At the same time, it is not so easy to put together our understanding of human beings as ends in themselves with our understanding of them as means. And the latter seems just as necessary as the former. Aristotle seems more bothered than Kant by the need to account for the natural inequality among men.

It is well to remember that the strong teleology was introduced for the purpose of making clear the naturalness of the household, and ultimately of the *polis*. That the ultimate result of this teleology should be cannibalism is simply Aristotle's way of making clear that, however natural the household may be, by itself its attempt to realize its nature leads to the most awful of crimes. That the pursuit of the simply good leads to the monstrous is a formula for tragedy. The household, by itself, is tragic.

It is instructive that Aristotle should have called the rule of a husband over his wife political. On the surface, this seems to indicate the possibility of political rule prior to the existence of the *polis*. In fact, however, it suggests that prior to the *polis* there are no husbands and wives. By itself, the household cannot preserve the distinction between wife and slave. A woman, like a slave, will be understood in terms of her use value. It is no accident that in his discussion of the natural superiority of men to women, Aristotle should have used the word *kreitton* (1254b14), meaning "better," but originally "stronger." *Kreitton* could only come to mean better in the *polis*; in the household it means only stronger. That a woman has a "place" in the home is at first presented by Aristotle as the condition for the possibility of female virtue. But failing any larger association in which she is recognized as "a half part of the free" (1260b18–19), her position will be so fully determined as to leave her without any freedom at all. The cyclops eats men and rules wife and children with an iron hand.

The sign of this difficulty is that Aristotle is unwilling to prescribe the kind of education necessary to women (and to children) independent of the regime in which they live. As their tasks (*erga*) will vary depending on the kind of regime, so will their virtues vary. Aristotle's use of the word *ergon* here is particularly suggestive. In the *Nicomachean Ethics* (1197b22–1198a20), it is on the basis of the *ergon* of human beings as human that Aristotle formulates his definition of virtue. Human beings are the animals with *logos*— speech or reason. The proper task of the species is the good use of this distinctive faculty. Human virtue is consequently the rational activity of soul. That the virtue of women and children is said to be regime-dependent, and so variable, suggests that they are being defined functionally and therefore considered not as human but solely as parts of a larger whole. This strong teleology is peculiarly indistinguishable from mechanism. A part understood wholly as a part has no value in its own right.[10]

That the young will come "to share in the regime" (1260b19–20) is the sign of why their education must be regime-dependent. There can be no education of children understood only as members of a household, for such an education would prepare them only for perpetual inferiority—natural slavery. Children can avoid the status of permanent minority only because of their positions as potential citizens. Otherwise, their alternatives would be either servility or rebellion. Without the city, growing up means parricide. Once again, the household apart from the city, precisely by trying to perfect itself through the perfection of its parts, would result in tragedy.

There are two indications that Aristotle is aware of this problem. At the very end of Book 1 (1260b13), he says that "every household is part of a *polis*," thereby indicating that the "households" existing prior to the *polis*, from which it grows, are not really households. A household can only be a household within the city, not because it is incomplete without the city, but because it is too complete. Secondly, and perhaps by this time not surprisingly, Aristotle uses a very peculiar quotation to support his claims about the role of women in the household. He quotes Sophocles' *Ajax* (1.293): "To a woman, silence brings proper order [*kosmon*]" (1260a31). The speaker is Tecmessa, the wife of Ajax. But she became his wife only after being captured in battle. Tecmessa is a war prize whose current "husband" is responsible for the death of her previous family. She is therefore also his slave. Tecmessa, in the midst of an account of how Ajax left their tent on the night he attempted to murder the entire Greek army in its sleep, tells his men how she attempted to dissuade him and was told to mind her own business and play the proper role of a woman. There are a number of ironies. Tecmessa is of course not remaining silent while she relates her tale. If Ajax was right about the role of women, she is wrong to speak. However, all indications are that she is not only right to speak, but that if Ajax had heeded her speech of the night before, he would not have made the biggest blunder of his career. All of this would have remained perfectly invisible, and with it Tecmessa's real virtues as a human being, had she remained silent, and so "orderly." A *kosmos* where everything is perfectly in its place has no place in it for human beings.

The simplest reason for the emphasis on property in Book 1 is now perhaps clearer. The *Politics* begins with the question of the naturalness of the *polis* understood as the comprehensive and sovereign human association. This proves to require that nature be understood teleologically. But to our surprise, a strict teleology turns out to be indistinguishable from a strict mechanism. Aristotle hints at their identity when he says that nature provides us with the nourishment we need, calling it property (1256a18–19), and then goes on to cite as an example the way in which the viviparous species provide their offspring with "the nature called milk" (1256b14–15). Nature, the perfect provider, is not distinguishable from nature, the product. In a world where nothing is understood in terms of itself, everything is "of" something else. But this is simply another way of saying that everything is a piece of property. Book 1 of the *Politics* points to the fact that in a world where the household, the *oikia*, was understood as the complete human association, human beings would be understood as *ktêmata*, pieces of property. Politics would be economics, and genuinely human life would be impossible.

The *polis* can be said to grow from the *oikia*, but not in a particularly benign sense. The household is an association for the sake of life, but as it becomes more and more perfect in its pursuit of life, it threatens to destroy the possibility of human life. The *polis* is the solution to this difficulty. Without it, the household tends toward cannibalism—the inability to recognize the human. The *polis* is therefore the means whereby tragedy is avoided. Aristotle spends so much time on property in Book 1 because only here does he provide some sense of how the growth of the *polis* occurs.

How exactly does it happen that the *polis*, which is instituted for the sake of living (*zên*), comes to be for the sake of living well (*eu zên*)? We get a hint from Aristotle's analysis of the art of the household, *oikonomikê*, which divides into a part dealing with the use of property within the household and a part, less properly speaking economic, dealing with the acquisition of property, *khrêmatistikê*. *Khrêmatistikê* in turn divides into a part that is natural, because dealing with the acquisition of property necessary for the efficient working of the household, and a part that is unnatural, because concerned not so much with the use value of property as with its value as exchangeable for other things. This less natural part in turn divides into a more natural part, dealing with the exchange of one product for another of use to the household, and the least natural part, concerned simply with property for its exchange value and for the unlimited accumulation of wealth understood as money.

One might expect Aristotle to understand the unnatural form of *khrêmatistikê* as a part of the art only by analogy—as a deviant and defective form. And yet Aristotle makes clear that it is "justly called *khrêmatistikê*" (1256b41). This reminds us of an earlier distinction, according to which human beings are political by nature because they alone have *logos*, and so they alone have the capacity to indicate the good and the bad and the just and the unjust. At the time the good and the just seemed identical, but perhaps they differ. As for the natural form of *khrêmatistikê*, Aristotle says that it deals with the use of property in a way "proper" to it—the word used is *oikeia*. The household use of things is the use of them as conforming to what they are. Shoes are meant to be worn to protect the feet. Only this use of them is *oikeia*. Ironically, the proper use of a piece of property, e.g., shoes, is to use it for some end other than itself. We recall that the proper being of property is to be "of another." The natural and proper (*oikeia*) use of property is its use in the household; this use is teleological. An article of property is understood in terms of its *telos*, its purpose or good. So natural *khrêmatistikê* seems to have to do with the human capacity to distinguish the good from the bad. Are we to take as a hint Aristotle's remark about the justice of calling the unnatural form *khrêmatistikê*? What might be just about trade for profit, banking, and usury?

The connection between the natural and the unnatural forms of *khrêmatistikê* seems to be growth. As soon as there is property, the possibility for both is present.

> For of each piece of property the use is dual, and both [uses] according to itself (*kath'auto*) but not similarly *kath'auto*. But one is proper (*oikeia*) and the other not proper to the thing. (1257a6–8)

A shoe has its natural use, and that is proper to it. The unnatural use of the shoe for exchange is different from the natural use, but only because the shoe has a natural use can it be used for exchange. Property may have two uses, but it has them both by virtue of being what it is *kath'auto*. The natural use is in a way despotic. A shoe must be kept in its place; it is always used for the sake of something else—a foot. But the natural use can never be separated from the possibility of the unnatural use. Whatever is worth using is worth exchanging. Consequently, it is not difficult to see how the unnatural use of property would grow in some sense "naturally" from the natural use. Shoes were not made for barter, but once one has them, one cannot help but see that they could be used for barter. Aristotle says one cannot barter in one's own household (although he was obviously not thinking of children when he said it). And even barter for necessities between households within villages is not "against nature" (1257a29). But from this sort of barter, the other, i.e., the unnatural sort, reasonably came to be or grew (*ek mentoi tautês egenet'ekeinê kata logon*). So the unnatural *khrêmatistikê* grows *kata logon*—according to speech or reason—even though *para phusin*—contrary to nature. This growth cannot occur within the household, or even within the village. It therefore requires something larger than either, the *polis*.

What fuels this growth, according to Aristotle, is the unlimited desire for life (1257b41–1258a2). Men make the mistake of thinking that the unlimited desire for life can be satisfied by an unlimited accumulation of the conditions for life. As a consequence, something necessary and natural to the household, the natural *khrêmatistikê*, develops into something that forces men beyond the household. Men enter the *polis* for reasons that are, properly speaking, of the household. Nevertheless, by so doing, they free themselves from the potential tyranny of the household. They think they seek in the *polis* something of the same order as what they sought in the household; they think they seek the good understood as the useful for life. What they discover is the necessary condition for the good life—freedom. This is what Aristotle means by distinguishing between the just and the good, and so between the *polis* and all other associations.

This distinction between the good and the just is prefigured by Aristotle's distinction between the two kinds of *khrêmatistikê*. One treats property always as a means to some further end; it treats it teleologically. Ironically, the unnatural *khrêmatistikê* treats pieces of property not in terms of what they are for, but as ends in themselves. The pursuit of money for its own sake is unnatural, but it provides an escape from the enslavement that is the necessary consequence of the perfectly natural association. The *polis*, therefore, is according to nature in a very peculiar sense. It is not natural in the sense of the household. Indeed, this will be Aristotle's criticism in Book 2 of the regime outlined by Socrates in Plato's *Republic*. To be natural, the city cannot be a perfect whole. The perfection of the whole would preclude the freedom of the parts. The household is what it is because it exists within a *polis*; to attempt to model the *polis* on the household is to make the mistake of thinking the household would remain what it is without the restraint of the *polis*. Aristotle criticizes the explicit teaching of the *Republic* for not taking into account that, in a city where every woman of a certain age is your mother, you will in fact have no mother. That incest is possible but undiscoverable in Socrates' regime means that there is no tragedy. There is no discoverable distinction between the good, understood as the useful, and the just. But this is to say that there are no human beings in Socrates' regime. For Aristotle, according to whom nature never makes something with a dual purpose, does not mean to say that we have *logos* in order to make clear the useful and harmful and also the just and the unjust. He means, rather, that the purpose of logos is to make it possible to indicate the useful and the harmful so as (*hôste*) also to indicate the just and the unjust. It is by *indicating* the use of things that we come willy-nilly to the question of justice and injustice. This is what it means for the household to grow into the *polis*.

Book 1 of the *Politics* raises the question of whether the *polis* is by nature. In an attempt to avoid the too-facile reply of our age that it is not, we may tend to underestimate the problematic character of Aristotle's claim that it is. Man cannot be a political animal by nature unless it is natural for him to rule and be ruled. But rule can only be natural to men if it is possible for them to be ruled and at the same time remain men. The goal of rule is always that the thing or person ruled should do what is good. But what is good for men is that they should do what is good willingly. Otherwise, they become slaves—mere instruments. The *polis* therefore points in two directions. As the sovereign human association, it is the one that aims at the highest good for men. It aims at happiness understood as doing what is best for you. As the comprehensive human association, it aims at happiness understood as freedom. Rule, even when it is the best possible rule (perhaps especially then), dehumanizes men. This is the importance of the natural slavery argument in Book 1.

Still, it is good for the good to rule. The naturalness of the *polis* is therefore threatened by its two functions. What does this mean, then, for man, the political animal?

> For whenever from a multitude some one common thing is put together and comes to be, whether from things brought together or things separated, in all there appears a ruler and a ruled, and from all of nature [or perhaps "from the nature of the all"] this is present in living things. For there is also a ruling principle in those things not participating in life, such as harmony. . . . But first, animals are put together from soul and body, of which the former is by nature ruler and the latter ruled. . . . And it is, as we say, first possible in animals to see both despotic rule and political rule. For the soul rules the body according to despotic rule, and the mind rules the appetites politically and royally. (1254a28–b6)

Soul rules as master over slave; mind rules politically over the appetites. The problem for man is, therefore, identical to the problem for the *polis*. When the *polis* is ruled like a household, citizens are ruled despotically and are no longer men. When the appetites are ruled despotically, a full half of our natures is suppressed. We become whole at the expense of our natures. The fulfillment of our nature becomes the suppression of our nature. If the task of the *Politics* is to show how the *polis* can be natural without being a perfect whole, its task is also to show how man can be natural without being a perfect whole. The question is whether an account can be given of human life as good while retaining its character as human.

Book 1 of the *Politics* does not solve this problem but raises it in terms of the household and identifies the *polis* as the location of its solution. The household avoids tragedy because of the existence of the *polis*. The *polis* prevents the good of the household from being the final good and so makes it possible for it to be really good. But the problem of the perfectly teleological association re-emerges on the level of the *polis* itself. It is the principle behind Aristotle's criticisms of his predecessors in Book 2. Book 3 begins with the *polis* as a community of citizens. In this way, it emphasizes the egalitarian element of any association. But bit by bit, this egalitarian element is eroded until, by the end of the book, Aristotle has said that kingship is the best form of rule when one man is preeminent in virtue, that the *polis* is really for the benefit or good of the best men in it, and, finally that kingship is not really political at all but like the rule of a father over a household. The best political order is not political, and its citizens are not fully human. The city, like man, is a class jumper.

The *Politics* as a whole is an attempt to find an alternative to the conclusion we are forced to draw at the end of Book 3 that the good *polis* would have to be a seemingly impossible mixture of the hierarchical and the egalitarian, of teleology and freedom. The problem is easier to specify than its solution. Like the household, Book 1 appears at first refreshingly wholesome. But like the household, its hidden power is that it sets the problem for what will come after.

This coincidence of form and content is not accidental. When Aristotle suggests at 1254a31–34 that the subject of "all of nature" or perhaps of "the nature of the all" might belong to a more exoteric discourse, he implies that the *Politics* is an esoteric discourse. We have accumulated considerable evidence to this effect, but why must the *Politics* be esoteric? Exoteric writing rules over us in the way that a master rules over a slave.[11] By simply revealing to us what we are to learn, it deprives us of the possibility of learning for ourselves. Writing that suggests but does not say directly, that rules without depriving those whom it rules of their humanity, is Aristotle's model for political rule.

There is another piece of evidence to this effect. An additional peculiarity of Book 1 is the extended anecdote Aristotle tells about Thales, the first philosopher. Thales' knowledge of the heavens allowed him to predict a good olive harvest and subsequently to corner the market on olive presses. He did all of this to show that philosophers could make money if they wished, but that most of the time they simply did not care to. Aristotle introduces this feat of Thales as exemplary of the unnatural *khrêmatistikê* (1259a5–18).

Is there then a connection between philosophy and the unnatural *khrêmatistikê*?

Philosophy means using things in an "unnatural" way. Consider the way in which Aristotle uses shoes as examples. In making them stand for a kind of thing he does something in a way very much like what a merchant does when accumulating shoes to sell. The merchant does not think of using these shoes for his feet or, indeed, for the feet of anyone he knows. He has, rather, had to think in his way about the necessity of protection in general for feet in general—i.e., to think about shoes in general. To think of a thing as exchangeable is to be at a second remove from seeing it as "good." It is to reflect on its goodness. Since this reflection on goodness seems only to be possible in an imperfectly ordered whole, as we have seen, the condition for the unnatural *khrêmatistikê* is the same as the condition for the *polis*. Our reflective nature, our being the animals with *logos*, makes the movement from *oikia* to *polis*, from the good to the just, in some sense quite natural. What comes as something of a surprise is that what makes the *polis* possible is also what makes philosophy possible. The two issues run parallel in Aristotle's *Politics* because philosophy—not philosopher-kings but the nature of philosophy—provides the model for Aristotle's understanding of the best regime. It seems proper, then, that the form of the *Politics* should mirror its content. Book 1 prepares us for the rest of the *Politics* in the same way that the household prepares us for the *polis*.

Chapter Two

Parricide and Politics:
Politics Book 2

The second book of the *Politics* seems not so much to advance Aristotle's own argument as to clear the way of competing alternatives. As a survey of regimes (*politeiai*) in theory and in practice it does not seem to have, or to need, a unifying principle other than to point out the defects of each regime considered. Nevertheless three things prove rather odd about the second book. In Book 1 Aristotle remarks on his procedure that

> if, as in other things so also in these, one should look at things growing naturally from the beginning, in this way one would theorize beautifully. (1252a24–26)

Fair enough—he then proceeds to trace the development of the *polis* from its beginning in the household. But then close to the outset of the second book he announces that "a first beginning must be made which is by nature the beginning of this inquiry" (1260b35–36). A first beginning? In Book 2? Now, the different beginnings may simply signal different things begun. Perhaps the natural beginning of political life (Book 1) is not the same as the natural beginning of the inquiry into political life (Book 2). And it is surely no accident that, while in Book 1 the issue is the *polis*, from Book 2 on it will be the *politeia*.[12] It is probably also significant that this second "first beginning" has to be *made* whereas in Book 1 Aristotle began with what we *see* in all *poleis*. Still, it is hard not to wonder about this second "first" beginning. The first peculiarity of Book 2, then, is that it is not Book 1.

The second odd thing has to do with Aristotle's criticism of Plato. About the most extraordinary feature of his teacher's account, the rule of philosoper-kings, Aristotle is altogether silent. He seems not so much to criticize the *Republic* as his own selective abridgement of Book 5. Furthermore, despite his own coupling of Socratic speeches with mimes (*Poetics* 1447b9–11), here Aristotle seems to treat them as though they were altogether contextless and unironic. For example, he criticizes Socrates' regime both for its goal—making the city most one—and for failing to achieve that goal since beneath the appearance of one city there will be two perpetually at odds with one another (1264a25–28), and yet the language in which Socrates initially introduces communism of property at the end of Book 3 (his ambiguous use of *hê allê polis* at 417b to mean either the rest of the city or the other city) tacitly acknowledges the problematic unity of his city. Only a few lines later in an outburst at the beginning of *Republic* Book 4, Adeimantus makes the whole issue explicit by demanding to know what's in it for the guardians in this city which is supposed to be theirs. Aristotle doesn't seem to acknowledge any of this. The extent to which a dramatic presentation of the words of an ironic man leaves room for self-criticism seems altogether to escape him.

Now one suspects, given his introductory remarks, that Aristotle knows his criticism will seem unfair.

> Since we intend to theorize about the political community which is best of all for those able to live as one would most pray for, we ought to inquire into other regimes (*politeiai*)—both those some of the cities said to be well governed use and if any others happen to have been well spoken of and seem to be beautiful (*kalon*—noble)— in order that what is right and useful may be seen. And further, that to seek something different from them may not seem wholly to be a form of wishing to be clever/to speculate (*sophizesthai*), but that we may seem to embark on this way of inquiry because those now existing are not beautiful. (1260b27–36)

Aristotle cautions us lest we interpret his attempt to distinguish his teaching as an attempt to distinguish himself. Pointed questions point as much to the questioner as to the questioned. Having pointed out that unfair criticism might be motivated by love of honor, Aristotle launches into what seems a manifestly unfair criticism of his teacher, Plato. This intellectual parricide is the second peculiarity of Book 2.

The third of the oddities of the second book has to do with its structure. It divides into three parts—discussions of theoretical accounts of the best *politeia* (2.1–8), of existing regimes reputed to be well ordered (2.9–11), and of legislators and their legislation (2.12). The first of these again divides into three—Aristotle's accounts of Plato (2.1–6), Phaleas (2.7) and Hippodamus (2.8), as does the second—his accounts of Sparta (2.9), Crete (2.10) and Carthage (2.11). The third is more difficult to divide (we will return to it later) but on its face seems to divide into a section distinguishing those who put forward something concerning the regime into private men, legislators and legislators who also crafted regimes, a section in which Solon stands as an example of the last group, and finally a series of shorter accounts of those who were simply legislators. The account of Plato in the first part then also divides in three—discussions of the community of women and children (2.2–4), of the community of property/*ousia* (2.5) and of Plato's *Laws* (2.6). And so on. . . . As figure 1 indicates, for Aristotle in Book 2, if it is worth saying, it is worth dividing into three, even at the expense of a certain artificiality. For example, Aristotle attacks Hippodamus first in a section combining a discussion of the division of the population into artisans, farmers and warriors and the division of land into sacred, public and private, second in a section on court reform, and finally in a section on the proposal to reward innovations. That Aristotle could easily have added a fourth is clear from Book 7 (1330b21–32) where he attacks Hippodamus for proposing that private homes be laid out in a regular fashion in the city, something he mentions, but allows to pass in Book 2 (1267b22–23).

What makes all of this so very odd is that this obsessive division of things into three is just what Aristotle is so hard on poor Hippodamus for.[13] Aristotle ridicules Hippodamus as rather odd (*perittoteros*) due to his love of honor or ambition. His way of life combines Spartan long hair, expensive ornament (*kosmos*) and cheap all purpose clothing that he didn't change according to the season. Hippodamus apparently is one of those men who have very little sense of what is appropriate when, where and with what. This seems to be connected with his willful division of the population into classes according to their functions without stopping to consider that,

Figure 1: Triplicity in Book 2

I. *politeiai* in speech
    A. Plato (2.2-6)
        1. community of women and children (2.2-4)
        2. community of property (2.5)
        3. *Laws* (2.6)
    B. Phaleas' failure to make the necessary
       three-fold division of the cause of stasis (2.7)
        1. desire for necessary things (cure: minimum
          of property)
        2. desire for superfluous things (cure:
          moderation)
        3. desire for pure pleasure without pain
          (cure: philosophy)
    C. Hippodamus (2.8)
        1. Hippodamus' regime
            a. divides population in three
                i.   artisans
                ii. farmers
                iii. warriors
            b. divides land in three
                i.   sacred
                ii. publilc
                iii. private
            c. divides law in three
                i.   *hybris*
                ii. harm
                iii. death
        2. reforms for existing law
            a. court reform
            b. rewarding innovation
            c. orphans
         3. Aristotle's attack on Hippodamus
II. existing "well-ordered" *politeiai* (2.9-11)
    A. Sparta (2.9)
        1. defects of household management
            a. slaves
            b. women
            c. property
         2. defects of political institutions
            a. ephors
            b. *gerousia*
            c. kingship
         3. defects of the fundamental principle
          of the regime
    B. Crete (2.10)
        1. Crete vs. Sparta
        2. defects of Crete
        3. what saves Crete
    C. Carthage (2.11)
        1. general comparison to Crete and Sparta
        2. specific comparison to Sparta
        3. defects of the regime
            a. common to all three
             b. democratic
             c. oligarchic
III. legislators (2.12)
    A. division of those speaking out (2.12.1)
    B. Solon (2.12.2-6)
    C. others (2.12.6-14)

for example, every member of any of the classes would, as human being, have to be a consumer as well as a producer. For Hippodamus the city is a city of functions, of arts, not a city of human beings. Aristotle suggests, but does not quite say, that Hippodamus' error has something to do with his being the first of those not involved in politics who attempted to speak about the best regime. He is an essentially private or apolitical man. This in turn seems to be connected to his wish to be learned concerning the whole of nature. Like the Pythagoreans, Hippodamus seems to begin with the importance of the number three.[14] He is a city planner who starts with a mathematical grid into which he fits everything else.

Aristotle's attack on Hippodamus calls attention to itself because of its atypical immoderation and its *ad hominum* character.[15] In calling attention to itself, however, it also calls attention to Aristotle's own procedure. Aristotle seems to be guilty of precisely what he finds so foolish about Hippodamus. This third odd thing about Book 2 seems connected to at least one of the others. Aristotle singles out Hippodamus as being *perittoteros*. Earlier he had singled out "all the speeches of Socrates" as possessing the *peritton*, adding that it was perhaps difficult for everything to be done beautifully (*kalôs*) (1265a11–13). And earlier still he had singled out *peritta* as one of those words like 'both', 'all' and 'even' which are necessarily ambiguous in their meaning (1261b29–30). Aristotle criticizes Hippodamus as being odd or eccentric and praises the speeches of Socrates (that is, Plato's dialogues) as being extraordinary (even though perhaps it is understandable that they do not do everything at once), but the praise and the blame are literally the same. If we wish to understand the apparent unfairness of Aristotle's criticism of Plato (our second puzzle) perhaps it would be useful to take a closer look at his strange self-criticism in the Hippodamus section (our third puzzle). Then we might be able to see Aristotle's intent in Book 2 as a whole (our first puzzle), for if he proves as guilty as his predecessors, then surely he has invited us to treat him in the same way he has treated them.

Aristotle criticizes Hippodamus for dividing things that are not really divisible so as to give the illusion of mathematical precision. Hippodamus divides the citizen body into farmers, artisans and warriors without ever indicating what underlies their discrete functions that makes them all equally citizens of the regime. There is thus nothing to prevent his farmers and artisans from being reduced to slaves and nothing to prevent his warriors from seizing the whole city. Similarly Hippodamus divides the land into plots according to the ultimate use of the crops harvested, as though a different kind of land were necessary to produce a different kind of crop for sacred, public and private use. Failing to see that the produce of one plot could be divided for three purposes is like failing to see the common humanity underlying the determination of functions of individual men in the city. Earth is not simply defined by the function for which men use it. The being of things is never univocal; things are not *eidê*.

Hippodamus' impatience with the imprecision of things is also at the root of his court reform. His suggestion at first seems reasonable. Judges should not be forced to condemn or acquit, but, since every action is in some way idiosyncratic, those who judge should have the option of defining some position in between the two extremes—on the one hand guilty on the other hand not. Otherwise they would have to forswear themselves by judging either one way or the other (1268a5–7). Presumably this means that it is not just to judge one way or the other, for the truth is always somewhere in between. While this principle may be true, Hippodamus fails to see how dangerous it is. As all the in-between positions are intelligible only as degrees of the two extremes, the denial, in principle, of simple guilt and innocence would ultimately undermine the very notion of a general rule, and therefore of its violation—crime, and so of trials altogether. If law cannot be general it cannot be, and without law there is no *polis*. Hippodamus does not see that particular action can be *understood* as particular only as an exception to a rule, as a modification of the general. His insistence on precision therefore threatens to render the city dumb. Law is the means whereby a city talks to itself about what it understands to be good and bad. This *logos* is necessarily imprecise. However, without it, or something like it, the city would become at best a beehive—everyone doing what he ought, but no one knowing what he was doing.

If Hippodamus' mistake is to demand too much precision, it seems strange to claim that his proposals would lead to the self-ignorance of the city. After all, it is here that Aristotle first uses the expression "political science" in the *Politics* (1268b37–38). It might seem more appropriate to say that Hippodamus underestimates the tension between a precision (proper to science and the arts) leading to unending revision and the need for stability in the law.[16] A political science modelled on the other sciences would have to aim at truth about political life, but unlike other sciences it would not be possible for it to exist apart from that of which it was the science. The movements of astonomers are not subjects of the science of astronomy, but *politikê* is itself necessarily part of political life. And yet the effect of its presence is to destabilize political life. Thus, while Hippodamus failed to see that there was a tension between political knowledge and political action, his political science still seems to be science.

It is still more complicated than this, however. Hippodamus was the first who did not participate in politics to attempt to say something about the best regime. He comes forward as a private man as though politics could be looked at from the outside, but part of Aristotle's ridicule is to accuse him of doing what he does for the sake of ambition—*philotimia*. Hippodamus has motives other than the pure pursuit of truth, and they infect his view of politics. His plan to reward innovations is, after all, a sort of self-glorification. A genuine political science, an account of what is distinctively political, would have to explain what underlies the tension between art and law, knowledge and politics. It would have to be a rational account of the imperfectly rational character of political life. The question is whether such a science is possible.

Aristotle criticizes Hippodamus for separating things that are not really separate; this overprecision is, in turn, connected to Hippodamus' ignorance of the tension between knowledge and politics. The problematic status of political self-knowledge is the overarching issue of *Politics* Book 2, which is concerned with regimes which have been *said* to be well governed and with those who have *spoken* about the best regime. From different directions, political science and lawgiving both point to what it means to talk about the political order from within the political order. This is borne out in various ways in the sections of the book we have not yet discussed.

In order to avoid *stasis*—internal political strife—Phaleas thought it sufficient to equalize the distribution of property—*ousia* (which also means being). And yet all could be equally impoverished, and still the result would not be political stability. Not property but desire would have to be equalized. And men do not only desire necessities. *Stasis* results as much, and probably more, from love of honor (*philotimia*—of which Hippodamus is guilty) as from hunger.[17] To equalize desires requires not only property redistribution but education. That is, political stability is a function not just of being or property (*ousia*) but also of seeming or reputation (*doxa*). Phaleas did not understand the extent to which the city *is* its self-understanding.

Plato, as always, is a more complicated case. Much of Aristotle's criticism turns on the fact that the communism of the *Republic* in creating conditions under which it would be impossible not to be virtuous also creates conditions under which it would be impossible to be virtuous. For example, while the motive underlying the communism of property is generous, communism itself makes generosity impossible by making it necessary and not voluntary.

> It is apparent then that it is better for possessions to be private (*idias*), but to make them common with respect to use. That they may become such, this task is peculiar (*idion*) to the legislator. (1263a38–41)

If the goals of legislation are always "private to the legislator," then the city will be experienced differently by those who make the laws and those who are subject to them.[18] The most extreme case is the legislators of the *Republic*—Socrates, Glaucon and Adeimantus—who in a way reserve all of virtue for themselves. It is they who have the thoughts underlying institutions like the communism of property. The citizens of their city only perform the deeds. Aristotle's criticism is thus always of Socrates and never of Plato since what he objects to (and in this he is not so far from Plato) is the regime outlined by Socrates and not the dialogue that gives rise to the regime—the republic and not the *Republic*. Socrates' republic may be subject to the same sort of criticism as Phaleas', but Plato's dialogue, the *Republic*, corrects it in the same way that Aristotle here corrects his predecessors.

Even this, however, is not quite correct. By introducing philosophy into the *Republic* in Book 5 Socrates makes an issue of whether the activity in which they have been engaged in the dialogue can be made a part of the city they are constructing. Everything turns on whether the philosophy they are describing is an adequate description of what they are doing as they describe it. Aristotle, of course, leaves out this famous third wave of Book 5 altogether and seems to substitute for it a discussion of Plato's *Laws*. Law seems at first to be the political substitute for living intelligence. But, the most part of the *Laws* being laws, he has said little concerning the *politeia*, and wishing to make it more shareable among *poleis*, by bits he turns it around (*periagei*) again toward the other *politeia*. (1265a1–4)

So the regime of the laws undergoes a *periagôgê*, a conversion, which brings it progressively closer to the regime of *the* regime, the *Republic*. Aristotle seems to mean that at the end of the *Laws* it becomes necessary to introduce the nocturnal council as a supplement to law. This *periagôgê*, then, like the one which frees the prisoners in the cave in *Republic* 7, is a sign that Plato knows that something like philosophy is an indispensable element of any *political* order. In the *Laws*, thinking cannot be purged from the city, but even in the perfect regime of the *Republic* the thinking that goes on in the city is not the same as the thinking that makes the city possible.

In the three actual regimes examined by Aristotle in Book 2, this problem emerges in a slightly different manner. Sparta understands itself in terms of courage or manliness. Aristotle shows that the regime designed to foster the virtue of he-men ends up ruled by women. And the regime that requires enormous self-control and moderation ends up fostering self-indulgence and luxury. Throughout chapter 9 Aristotle plays on the double meaning of *arkhein*, to rule and to begin. The beginning rules in ways that are frequently unpredictable. One cannot understand Sparta without taking into account how it understands itself, but its self-understanding is a cause of its turning out differently from what it thinks it is.

The political institutions of Crete are cruder than those of Sparta, and so one would expect it to be less well governed. In fact Aristotle says that it is better governed for a strange (*atopos*) reason, its location (*topos*). It has more of the feel of a family because it is an island, and there is nowhere for those who are disenchanted to go and no outside ally to whom they can appeal for help. Now *topos* is the single thing Aristotle had claimed must be shared in any city (1260b41). Every *polis* has a *topos*, but no *topos* is simply a *topos*. The idiosyncracies of a particular location will always affect a *polis* in ways that are not simply traceable to its laws or its regime. Therefore its self-understanding as embodied in its laws will be out of sync with reality; this self-misunderstanding will, in turn, affect the reality of the *polis*. A genuine political science would have to take account of the effects of the *polis'* inevitable, but unpredictable, misunderstanding of itself. And to the extent that this political knowledge is to be transferred into practice, a legislator would have to know how to predict the unintended effects of laws and legislate accordingly. He would therefore seem to be legislating with one end in view but in fact his goal would be *idion* to him. The Cretan legislator who arranged it so that there would be little food at the common mess, that is, who legislated want or imperfection for the sake of a greater good, is said by Aristotle to "have philosophized" (1272a20–25). A wise legislator might devise an elaborate system of electing presidents not by popular vote but through an electoral college with the delegations from each state casting all of its votes for one candidate. His presumed motive might be to place an aristocratic check on pure democracy. His real motive might be to conceal narrow margins of victory thus enhancing the authority of democratic rule. Or, of course, the one could be an accidental result of the other.

Aristotle praises the Carthaginians for governing themselves beautifully (*kalôs*) and *perittôs*—in an extraordinary way. But the regime has an interesting defect. It is aristocratic insofar as it recognizes that rulers ought to be selected on the basis of their worth. But the Carthaginians also see that virtue requires leisure and leisure requires wealth. So they look both to wealth and to virtue in choosing leaders. Now elsewhere Aristotle is very clear about the relation between virtue and equipment.[19] What the Carthaginians say, then, is true, but the fact that they say it alters their regime. Leaders with a certain degree of wealth are not so subject to the necessities of the moment; the most wealthy are probably not as subject to bribery. But to make wealth a criterion of election makes it seem something desirable for its own sake. By stating the truth the Carthaginians turned their aristocracy into an oligarchy.

If Aristotle's criticisms of those who theorize about the best *politeia* as well as of existing *politeiai* all turn on the failure to understand the role that understanding plays in political life, what are we to make of his suggestion that he himself is subject to the same criticism? The crucial division of Book 2 is the division between those who speak out about the best regime and existing well governed regimes—the division between theory and practice. If Aristotle is like Hippodamus, he will have made the two more distinct than they really are. At 1266a31–32, for example, he refers to "the regimes of private men and those of philosophers and statesmen (*politikoi*)," clearly coupling the latter two. In the final chapter of Book 2 Aristotle divides those who have spoken out about the *politeia* into those not sharing in political action in any way but spending their lives as private men, those who are craftsmen of laws alone, and those who are craftsmen of both laws and of *politieai* (1273b27ff).[20] While we would expect Plato to be in the first class, Aristotle introduces him (along with Phaleas, but *not* Hippodamus) at 1274b9–10 as someone who introduced laws. Plato is of course literally *the* man who crafted *hoi nomoi* (*The Laws*) and *hê politeia* (*The Republic*), but he was not engaged in politics in any ordinary sense. Aristotle has thus gone out of his way to confuse the distinction between theory and practice with which he had begun Book 2.

In the second book of the *Politics* Aristotle moves from a discussion of the *polis* to a discussion of the *politeia*. The *politeia* is the form which determines the way of life of the *polis*. It is the Soviet regime but not mother Russia, the Fifth Republic but not France. If political inquiry means asking what principle governs how citizens share (*koinônein*) things in a community (*koinônia*), then the inquiry into the *polis* leads necessarily to the *politeia*. Only to the extent that the *polis* is essentially the *politieia* is political science possible, for only then is the *polis* a coherent whole. Now, if the *polis* were essentially the *politeia*, Hippodamus would be right. It would be possible to be a private man speculating on politics. The *polis* would be perfectly intelligible from the outside and *politikê epistêmê*—political science—would be like the other arts. But thinking about politics is not *idion*; it is constituted, and is affected, by political life. Politics is intrinsically philosophic; unlike bees in the hive part of what it means for us to live in the city is to ask what the best political order is. On the other hand, philosophy is intrinsically political. Hippodamus notwithstanding, the beings we inquire after are not fully comprehended by the designations we give them. Our humanity is not exhausted in our function—in a way, there is no such thing as a carpenter. Philosophy—asking what beings really are—means discovering precisely how our designations of them fall short. It is therefore necessarily parasitical and in the case of Aristotle, parricidical. He prefaced his attack on the *Republic* with a warning that his motives might seem impure. But if the only way to disclose the incomplete rationality of the *polis* is to treat it as rational (as the *politeia*) so as to be able to mark where it is not, and if this is in fact the procedure of Plato's *Politeia*, then in order to do what Plato did, Aristotle must imitate him rather than obey him.[21] By treating Plato's *Politeia* the same way he treats the *politeia* Aristotle points to the fundamental kinship between philosophy and politics.

Book 1 of the *Politics* is about the fact that political life begins when men think in general about the good—that is, they think about justice. Book 2 is about the fact that thinking is not simply separable from doing, and so it is in some way under the same constraints as doing. What makes it impossible for the *polis* to be the regime is the ineradicability of the accidental. This is what makes it necessary for Aristotle to criticize Plato. There is no straightforward doctrine revealing the power of the accidental. It shows itself only after the fact in the way things don't work. And this is the way we discover what things are.

Aristotle almost ends Book 2 with a reflection on Pittacus' laws concerning drunkenness. Pittacus made drunken men pay a greater penalty than sober men when a law was broken. By refusing to treat drunkenness as a mitigating circumstance he pays more attention to the action than to the intention behind it. In treating the effect rather than the cause, Pittacus takes account of the fundamental problem of Book 2—that intention (*politieia*) does not simply make things what they are. Or, the *polis* is a bit like a drunken man—it is goal directed, but in a very obscure way. "Political science" is therefore a bit like a science of drunkenness. For this reason the natural beginning of the *polis* is not the same as the natural beginning of the inquiry into the *polis*. Book 2 is not Book 1. It is one thing to seek a rational understanding of the incompletely rational and another to attempt its complete rationalization.

Book 2, of course, is not the end of the *Politics*. If Book 1 makes politics philosophic and Book 2 makes philosophy political, what remains to be seen is to what extent whatever perfection is intrinsic to philosophy can serve as a model for whatever perfection is intrinsic to political life. Not wisdom, but philosophy is Aristotle's paradigm for political life. The remainder of the *Politics* is the working out of this project.

Chapter Three

The Poverty of Philosophy:
Politics Book 3

Book 3 of the *Politics* is unusually aporetic. Aristotle discusses various issues at length only to leave them explicitly unresolved. He asks whether a newly formed regime is responsible for the actions of the oligarchy or tyranny that preceded it.[22] At stake is the question of the self-identity of the city over time. To ask when the city remains the same is to ask what it really is. After considerable argument, Aristotle seems to answer that the being of the city is its regime—its *politeia*. But rather than drawing what might appear the obvious conclusion—that a city under a new regime is not responsible for the acts of the previous regime—he says that this practical question of liability would require another account. The city apparently is and is not the regime. Book 3 also ends with an *aporia*. While the long argument concerning the relative merits of the rule of law and the rule of active intelligence (1286a8–1287b35) seems to prove the rule of law superior, it is immediately followed by the claim that the best regime is the rule of the best man (1288a32–b2).

Other issues, apparently resolved, might as well have been aporetic. At 1275a21–23, Aristotle defines a citizen "simply" (*haplôs*) as one participating in judging (*krisis*) and rule (*arkhê*). But this is an ambiguous "simply."—In Athens *krisis* and *arkhê* need mean no more than jury duty and magistracy. While their general sense does indeed point to something like full participation in the affairs of the city, their specific Athenian sense means much less. In Athens (as in New York City), one can be a juror or hold an office without exercising much judgment or rule. And in chapter 8, shortly after introducing what is on mathematical grounds supposed to be an exhaustive articulation of the variety of regimes into those in which one, few or many rule either well or badly, Aristotle announces that he wasn't altogether serious about democracy as the bad rule of the many and oligarchy as the bad rule of the few. The one is really the rule of the poor (*aporoi*), the other of the wealthy (1279b34–1280a2).

These *aporiai* leave unresolved issues of considerable practical importance. When is a city obligated to pay its debts? When is it just to ignore written law? Is there such a thing as partial citizenship? If wealth and poverty are the reality underlying oligarchy and democracy, how do we know there are not still other criteria of rule, and so how do we know Aristotle's classification of regimes is exhaustive? Book 3 seems to contain as many questions as it does answers. Perhaps we will be able to judge why by turning to the beginning.

> For him inquiring about the regime (*politeia*), both what each is and what sort, almost the first inquiry is to see concerning the city (*polis*), What ever is the city? (1274b31–33)

If you want the regime, you ask about the city, for the being of a thing is its form (*eidos*), and the regime (*politeia*) is the form (*eidos*) of the city (*polis*) (1276b1–10). While the same human beings might inhabit the same place under two different regimes, the two cities are apparently as different as the C major and A minor scales. Still, why is "What is the city?" *almost* the first question?— When at the outset of the *Oedipus at Colonus*, the aging Oedipus asks Antigone what the place is to which they have come, we expect her to say something like "Athens." It would have been queer for her to answer him by saying "Monarchy." Nevertheless, had he then asked her what Athens was, she might have said, "A monarchy." To do more than name the city in speech means to describe it as a member of a kind of which there may be, in principle, other members. But treating it in this way, as though its regime were its being, abstracts from the most ordinary feature of political life. For the citizen, his city is not one of a class; it is unique. He sings "America the Beautiful" or "Deutschland über alles," not "O Democracy." The first question is thus "What is *this* city?" not "What is *the* city?" Its answer is a proper name.

Granted, there must be a city to have an inquiry about the city. Nevertheless, the being of any city, unlike that of a family, in large measure consists in the way it has raised and answered the question of how men best live together. In Book 1 Aristotle was concerned with the transformation of a community of people working together for a common good (the family) into a community of people self-consciously working together for a common good (a political community). Book 1 therefore moved from the good as the guiding principle of familial life to the just as the guiding principle of political life. Man, the speaking animal, is also the political animal, because political life means not only acting teleologically but speaking teleologically; it means openly to hold (*nomizein*) something to be good. In this way political life is always life under law (*nomos*). The parts of the city with which Aristotle is concerned in Book 3 are not families but citizens, because it is the part of a citizen to rule and judge. A citizen is a self-aware member of a community. To say that the city is the regime, then, is to say that the question of the city, in a way, constitutes the city.

Book 3, which contains so many unanswered questions, begins with the assertion that the being of the city consists in raising the question, "What is the city?" The problem of the relation of city to regime comes up within political life as the question of the unity of the city over time. For what is the city to be held responsible? Those denying that the city remains the same regardless of changes in regime seem always to state their case in terms of the badness of the regime whose actions they wish to disown. If we want to renege on the debts of a previous regime, we call it an oligarchy or a tyranny.[23] Curiously, Aristotle omits democracy, later identified as one of the three defective regimes. Perhaps the city is more to be identified with the *dêmos*—the people—than with oligarchs or tyrants. Book 3 would then begin with a certain democratic bias. Now, Aristotle identifies poverty as the principle of democracy; the poor (the *aporoi*) are those who have *aporia* (poverty or want). Hence, in addition to containing an unusual number of unresolved *aporiai*—puzzles or questions—Book 3 begins with a suggestion that the being of the city is somehow the question or *aporia*, "What is the city?" and with a bias in favor of democracy, the principle of which is *aporia*, or poverty. The overarching question of Book 3

might, then, be put in the following way: What does *aporia* as question or puzzle in Aristotle's description of his own narrative have
to do with *aporia* as poverty, the principle of democracy as understood within Aristotle's narrative, and why is the connection between
the two so important for political life?[24]

Aristotle's turn from the question of the city to the question of
the citizen is his turn from "almost the first" to the first question.[25]
A city is made up of its citizens—those who in some way can be
said to rule. Who the citizens are will depend on the way the underlying principle of the regime justifies the rule of some over others. How a city answers the question, "Who are the citizens?" will
therefore point to the understanding of justice characterizing its
regime. Book 3 is concerned with adjudicating among the various
competing claims. Accordingly, it is also concerned with what regime is the best.[26]

At the same time, even this turn to the citizen is not so straightforward.

> For the city is a multitude of citizens so that it must first be inquired
> whom it is necessary to call citizen and who the citizen is. (1274b40–
> 1275a1)

What, precisely, is the relation between those who are citizens and
those who are called citizens? Does it imply a similar distinction
between what a regime is called and what a regime is?[27] Aristotle
seems to distinguish between real citizens and those ordinarily called
citizens. Hence, if citizens (those who share in judging and
ruling) vary according to the regime, whoever is called a citizen is
a citizen. If, however, "unjust" and "false" amount to the same
thing (1276a1), one unjustly a citizen would not be truly a citizen,
and an unjust regime would not be truly a regime. Only in a good
regime could a man be a citizen; everywhere else he would
merely be called a citizen. Two criteria are at odds here. According
to one, if justice is the measure of political life, only the most just
regime will be truly a regime. According to the other, there must
be something in everything we call a regime that justifies our
calling it a regime. The one is a measure of the goodness of
political life, the other of its intelligibility. The question is how the
two fit together. Not surprisingly this is what is at issue in Aristotle's account of when a city can be understood to remain the same
over time.

On the one hand, only the good city is a city; on the other, a bad city remains a city. This double criterion points directly to Aristotle's account of the variety of regimes. Regimes must either be ruled by one, few, or many; this division, neutral to the distinction between good and bad rule, preserves the plurality of kinds of regime. But Aristotle also divides regimes on the basis of their devotion to the common good; this division would ultimately force a ranking that would deny regime status to any but the best regime. The one is an eidetic account for the sake of making the distinctions among cities intelligible, the other a teleological account for the sake of understanding what a good city is. The *aporiai* of Book 3 all stem from Aristotle's insistence on putting the two together. The good does not fit together so easily with the true; the one subverts and the other clarifies conventional distinctions. The question is how to form a coherent whole of radical conventionalism and radical idealism.

Aristotle hints at the necessity for such a whole in his discussion of why neither its place nor the human beings inhabiting it sufficiently identifies a city.

> The account (*logos*) seems akin to this question (*aporia*): how at any time it is necessary to say the city is the same or not the same but different. Now, the most superficial inquiry into the question is about place and human beings. For it is possible for place and human beings to be unyoked with some making their home in one place and others in another. . . . Surely not by walls, for there could be one wall thrown up around the Peloponnese. Such perhaps (*isôs*) is Babylon, and any which has the outline rather of a nation than of a city. The capture of it, they say, at least, was not perceived by a part of the city for three days. (1276a23–30)

On the one hand, a city is not just anything that is called a city. On the other, if it took three days for parts of Babylon to hear that the city was conquered, was it conquered before that? A city is no more defeated before admitting defeat than a tyrant can rule without the tacit acquiescence of the people over whom he rules. It is therefore "looking to the regime that a city must be said to be the same" (1276b10–11)—"must be said" by us reading the *Politics* but also by those within the city. The regime is what gives those within the city a sense of the identity of the city; it is their common understanding of justice. The sameness of the city depends not just on the sameness of the regime but also on the opinion of those within the city that the regime is the same. This opinion is in fact constitutive of the regime. America has undergone a variety of radical changes since its European colonization, but only one, beginning with the Revolution and ending with the adoption of the Constitution, is thought sufficiently radical to be called a change in regime, and what is thought is all important. If every regime depends on what the city is thought to be, said to be, or called, then every regime is in some sense democratic. In the later discussion of law, Aristotle brings this point home powerfully.

> This is the beginning (*arkhê*) of the inquiry: whether it is more advantageous to be ruled by the best man or the best laws (*nomoi*). For to those holding (*nomizousi*) it to be advantageous to be ruled by a king, the laws (*nomoi*) seem to speak (*legein*) only the general, but not to command with regard to whatever crops up. (1286a8–13)

The advocates of kingship do not seem to realize that in holding (*nomizein*) that one needs a king to handle the idiosyncracies of particular circumstances, they are creating a kind of law (*nomos*). Only the king whose subjects never thought through the advantages of being ruled by a king would rule simply as a king. And such a rule would be despotic rather than political.[28] Insofar as political rule always requires some measure of consent, it is always to this extent democratic.

This initial democratic bias is undermined as Book 3 progresses. Aristotle moves to a discussion of the relation of the good citizen and the good man in chapters 4 through 5. By introducing the possibility of bad rule, he has also introduced the bad city. Now, since the being of a city is its regime, and a regime is what it is by virtue of who rules in it, in a bad city the bad will rule. In other words, in a bad city, a good citizen will be a bad man. The good city will be defined by the regime in which the good man is the good citizen—i.e., in which the one who is called good is good.[29] Aristotle never openly abandons this principle; indeed, he reaffirms it in the very last chapter of Book 3 (1288a37–39). And yet within the good city only the ruler can be a good man. Just as citizens in defective regimes are good only relative to their regimes (a good oligarch is not a good man), so also, given the heterogeneous tasks necessary for the existence of any city, even the best regime will have good citizens who are good relative only to the task they perform. Even the best city will need artisans and soldiers, but its good artisans and good soldiers are not for that reason identical to good men.

Aristotle goes so far as to suggest that because there are different senses of virtue, all good citizens might be said to share in virtue in some sense. Rulers and ruled would then share a common good. And since learning to be ruled is a necessary condition for learning how to rule—a general must really know what he is asking of his soldiers—they would in large measure share a common education. But does this not mean that all are taught to obey so that some will learn how to rule? If so, is this a common good, or is the city really for the good of some and not all? Aristotle acknowledges the problem but then unexpectedly justifies the rule of the man of extraordinary virtue by saying that it would be unnatural for the part to be preeminent over the all; this means, of course, that the whole has been identified with its highest element (1288a26–27). In addition, since certain sorts of work are necessary for the survival of the city but incompatible with living well, not even all of those human beings without whom there could be no city will be citizens. In all of these ways Aristotle has to acknowledge that there will be a difference between those who rule and those who are ruled. But the decisive issue is prudence for, although justice, courage, and moderation admit of versions in both rulers and ruled, "prudence (*phronêsis*) is not a virtue of one who is ruled, but true opinion" (1277b28–29). Thus, those who are ruled are not virtuous, for "it is clear . . . that it is not possible to be good in the highest sense without prudence."[30] It is not so much in their actions—their behavior—that good citizens must fall short of being good men but in their awareness of what they are doing.

We are therefore faced with the following difficulty. For rule to be political, those who are ruled must in some way assent to being ruled; political life is in this way fundamentally democratic. However, once we admit that there is some measure of political life according to which certain regimes are good and others not, the best regime will be the one in which the best rule. At first "the best" seem simply caretakers of those over whom they rule, but when the king becomes a shepherd his subjects begin to look like sheep. The rule of the best for the common good always threatens to become despotic rather than political. The principle of the former is the good of the ruler and of the latter the common good. Yet it is not altogether clear what this rule for the common good will entail. The common good is not simply what is commonly desired. It is rather a maximizing of the possibility for excellence or virtue. When virtue is understood to be rule, the common good will have to be the good of the rulers. In a regime taking as the standard of its goodness the good men it produces, the common good will end up meaning what is good for the best. Rule of the best will be for the best (1279a35–37). This "community" of rulers and ruled will depend on not too scrupulously analyzing what is meant when we say "it's all for the best." That is, it will depend on a false awareness on the part of those ruled. Political rule thus requires that the ruled be simultaneously aware and unaware. Its principles are at once democratic and aristocratic. This *aporia* at the heart of Book 3 is at the heart of politics altogether.

Aristotle first classifies regimes into those ruled well or badly by one, few, or many. Good rule by one is kingship, by a few is aristocracy, and by many is *politeia*—the word for all regimes standing also for a specific type. Bad rule by one is tyranny, by few is oligarchy and by many is democracy. As we have seen, oligarchy quickly gets reinterpreted as rule of the wealthy and democracy as rule of the poor (1279b6–10). This is particularly important in light of what seems a casual remark at 1278b10–15.

> For everywhere the government (*politeuma*) of the city is sovereign, and the regime is the government. I mean (*legô*), for example, in democracies the people is sovereign, but in oligarchies, on the contrary, the few. And we say that *politeia* is different from these. [or: "And we say another *politeia* to be of these."]

On the one hand this suggests that the specific form of regime called "regime," unlike democracy or oligarchy, is ruled neither by the many nor by the few. If this is correct, it clearly undermines Aristotle's categories of regime. On the other, the final sentence might mean that all other regimes are composed of oligarchy and democracy, the true principles of which are wealth and poverty. The fundamental political distinction would then be rich versus poor.[31] In fact, the sentence must be read both ways. Genuinely political life cannot be either simply democratic or simply oligarchic. But to say it must be a combination of the two is problematic. If a regime is not solely what the city is (its form or ordering principle) but also what it is called (what it is thought to be by the citizens who inhabit it), then mixing oligarchy and democracy would mean mixing together a self-image as poor with a self-image as rich. Rich versus poor is the most divisive of political distinctions because the most difficult to reconcile into the common self-image necessary for a single regime.

Aristotle ends chapter seven with this revision of his classification of regimes.

> For tyranny is monarchy looking to the advantage of the one ruling monarchically, oligarchy looking to that of the wealthy (*euporoi*) and democracy toward the advantage of the poor (*aporoi*), but none of them with a view to profiting in common. (1279b5–10)

He begins chapter eight as follows.

> One ought to speak at a little more length of what each of these regimes is. For there are also some questions (*aporiai*), and it belongs to the one philosophizing concerning each way of inquiry, and not only having a view to action, neither to overlook nor to omit anything but to make clear the truth concerning each. (1279b11–15)

The double meaning of *aporia* as question and poverty is coupled with Aristotle's introduction of philosophy. He goes on to alter his terminology, substituting *ousia*—property or substance—for *euporia*—wealth. *Ousia* is derived from *ousa*, the feminine participle in the present tense of the verb to be. It means property, but also being or substance—realty and reality. Aristotle uses it regularly to signify the object of the highest kind of philosophy— first philosophy or metaphysics.[32] Philosophy is experiencing an *aporia* about *ousia*. It is the truth of questioning—an apparently impossible mixture of ignorance and knowledge. For utter ignorance would make one unaware of what to ask, and utter knowledge would leave one with nothing to ask. As Aristotle's model for how to mix together *aporia* and *ousia*, poverty and wealth, philosophy is also his model for political life. It is a mixture of democracy and oligarchy. This is what it means to say that the question of the city is the city. Political life requires answers in the form of an understanding of justice embodied in its regime. At the same time, it must preserve the original questioning that gave rise to the embodiment of this understanding. Citizens must understand themselves as well-off if they are to be content with their regime, with its principles of justice, but must understand themselves as needy if they are to understand the justice of these principles. They must be simultaneously loyal and estranged. If the principles they live by are to remain visible to them, they must remain open questions.

The city is necessarily a heterogeneous community made up of a variety of groups, each having the potential to understand its rule as best for all. Faction is thus an inevitable temptation for every city. What any group, the poor or the well-born, for example, considers the wholeness of the all—its understanding of the regime—will depend on what the group is. In Book 3, Aristotle tries to understand the element of truth in the most common claims to rule. The heart of his argument concerns democracy and oligarchy, since poverty and wealth are the most difficult of the claims to reconcile.[33] The poor never justify their rule on the basis of their poverty. Their claim is rather that they are collectively better than the few, however constituted.

> It is possible for the many, each of whom is not a good man, nevertheless to be better when they combine than those [the good]— not individually but all together, as dinners brought together [are better] than those supplied from one expenditure. For, being many, each is able to have part of virtue and prudence, and, when they combine, the multitude, having many feet, many hands and many senses [is able] to become like one man and so also concerning character and thought. (1281a42–1281b8)

But is a human being organized democratically, as this argument seems to imply? Aristotle has not described a man here so much as an Aristophanic monster, which, lacking any hierarchical or ruling principle, is not a whole at all. There is something at once compelling and incomplete in the claim that men are wiser than any man because no man is "man."[34] The collective wisdom of the many is greater than that of the few in the way one inhabiting, and so using, a house knows more about it than the builder (1282a14–23). Lacking a principle of wholeness, this wisdom is essentially passive. Accordingly, the many cannot rule as a many; they can only respond to attempts to rule in accordance with some other principle. Because the many can rule in some ways but not in others, it becomes necessary to decide when they can and when they cannot. Even within the regime that is supposed to be founded on equality, some principle of justice is necessary other than arithmetic equality. Aristotle therefore turns to the problem of distributive justice in chapter 12.

While it is clear to all that the just is somehow the equal, it is not so clear what the equal is.

> But the just is the political good, and this is the common advantage. Justice seems to all to be something equal (*ison*). . . . For they say the just to be something for someone, and that it should be equal for equals. But one should not fail to notice of what sort of equality and inequality it is. For this contains a question (*aporia*) and political philosophy. (1282b16–23)

All regimes share this question or *aporia*: What is the equal? As long as the meaning of equality is unclear, justice remains unclear. Every regime must therefore raise and answer this question. Political philosophy, mentioned here for the only time in Aristotle's writings, is the art of measuring the just.[35] As with all arts, some will be skilled in it, others not. In this most important respect, political life cannot be democratic. The introduction of the notion of an art of justice forces the argument of Book 3 toward the question of kingship.

Book 3 began by reducing the question of the city to the question of the regime, and the question of the regime to the question, "Who is a citizen?" This amounts to asking what the ruling authority is in the city. But the ruling authority is defined by how it measures the equality that every city demands. In the best political order, the correct measurement of this equality prevails. The fundamental political question is therefore "What is the correct measurement of the equal?" The answer given to this question by any regime will be embodied in its laws (1282a42–1282b13).[36] But no law applies itself, and so

> the ruler, whether one or more, should be sovereign concerning those things about which the laws are altogether unable to speak precisely because it is not easy in general to be clear about everything. (1282b2–6)

In practice, asking for the correct measurement of the equal amounts to asking for the correct measurer of the equal. The fundamental political problem cannot finally be solved by institutions, but only by active intelligence because, in practice, justice requires more than a general answer to the question, "What is equal?" It requires someone who can answer the question. The unique introduction of political philosophy in chapter 12 points to this problem. The city does not need *a* political philosophy—that is to say, ideology. It needs political philosophy.

Aristotle demonstrates the limits of what we would call ideology by working through the various legitimate general claims to rule to show how each is finally problematic. While the majority has perhaps the strongest claim to be the city, the principle underlying its claim ultimately leads to tyranny. The poor begin by expropriating the property of the rich. Since, however, they justify their rule not by their poverty but by their numbers, and since this never changes (there will always be a majority), grounds will always exist for expropriation. Although differences of wealth may become less pronounced, they are not for that reason perceived as less important. If consistent, then, the majority will expropriate again and again, always purifying itself, until it finally becomes like a monster devouring itself. The rule of the rich is equally unstable. As a principle it demands either that the richest individual rule or that those with the most wealth collectively rule. The first would be tyranny, the second democracy. The rule of the free and well-born is an attempt to generate a hierarchic principle out of an underlying egalitarian principle. The principle of democracy is rule or citizenship of the free; the well-born are those who come from families whose members have been citizens for a very long time. Thus, there are the free and the *really* free. But this conventional claim to rule conceals a previous decision about who is entitled to citizenship, thus also concealing the real principle of the regime—the ground for this initial decision. Even the rule of the good unjustifiably dishonors the genuine contributions to the city from those who provide necessary conditions for its existence. Without wealth and numbers, there would be no city.

What is the solution to this *aporia*? It is necessary somehow to mix the various claims in a nondoctrinaire way to do justice to each. Any disproportionately large claim has to be eliminated, and any absolutely fixed claim will tend to become disproportionate.[37] Absolute freedom of speech has to be tempered on a case-by-case basis by judges who decide, for example, that it cannot apply to the man who falsely shouts "Fire!" in a crowded theater. To protect the city from their disproportionately large claim, the very wealthy must be exiled. Aristotle justifies ostracism with several metaphors. The first is illuminating; "For neither would a painter allow his animal a foot exceeding symmetry, not even if it should be distinguished with respect to beauty" (1284b7–10). Does the exile of a swollen foot mean the exile of Oedipus? Is the tragedy of political life that in the *polis* the man of disproportionate virtue somehow ceases to be virtuous?

How to identify the various claims about equality seems clear, but how does one measure one claim against another? They are so different as to be incommensurable. This sort of measuring cannot be done by formula; it requires judges on the spot, who, if they are to judge well, must be wise or prudent. At some level, then, the just city would need a disproportionately wise man. What would the city do with his claim for proportionate equality? Ostracism would be a tragedy for him. Making him an absolute judge—king— would be a tragedy for the city.[38] The good of the city sometimes requires unjust ostracism.[39] Ironically, the very act of deciding whom to ostracize makes one a candidate for ostracism.

The best regime needs political philosophy but cannot afford to acknowledge political philosophers. This is the fundamental *aporia* of political life. Aristotle indicates that it is best to avoid this sickness of the "swollen foot" by constructing a regime in advance so as to rule out the possibility of disproportionate greatness, but the "second sailing," he says, is to correct it after the fact (12184b17–20).[40] Now, if all regimes are necessarily problematic because either they have a wise man within them, and so are defective, or they do not, and so are defective, then all politics will necessarily be a second sailing. It will involve correcting exaggerated claims for justice.

All of this is connected to the final section of Book 3—Aristotle's analysis of kingship. He begins by hinting at the central difficulty: "It must be inquired whether it is advantageous to the city or land which is to be beautifully managed to be ruled by a king or not. . . ." (1284b37–39). Is what a king rules properly called a city at all? Aristotle lists five kinds of kingship. Spartan kingship amounts to military command together with certain religious duties; it can be hereditary or elected. Barbarian kingship is hereditary tyranny under law. An *aisumêtês* is a tyrant, elected either for life, for a set period of time, or for the accomplishment of a certain end. Heroic kingship is hereditary rule as a military commander, judge, and performer of religious rites.[41] Aristotle adds a fifth, almost as an afterthought.

But there may be a fifth form of kingship when one is sovereign over all, just as each tribe and each city is over the shared things, arranging things according to household management. For just as household management is a kingship of the household, pambasileia is household management of a city or tribe—one or several. (1285b30–34)

Having divided kingship into five types, Aristotle proceeds immediately to collapse the five into two, *pambasileia*—rule of the all-powerful king—and Spartan kingship (1285b34–35). He then argues that since the Spartan variety is a product of legislation, it is an office and not properly a form of kingship at all (1287a3–4). Thus, there seems to be only one form of kingship—*pambasileia*, previously described as a form of household management. But the *Politics* literally begins with the claim that political rule and household management are different in kind (1252a8–15). There seems to be no form of kingship as political rule.

The remainder of Book 3 is an extended warning about the dangers of kingship, measured in comparison to the rule of law. Aristotle reminds us that one man is more easily corrupted than many (1286a31–35), that, in any case it would be better for a group of good men to rule rather than one man (1286a35–1286b8), that it is difficult for even a good monarch to resist handing his rule over to his children, who are probably not as good as he (1286b25–27), that law as "mind without desire" better satisfies the need for disinterested rule (1287a31–32), and so on. Still, as Aristotle is aware, none of this solves the problem of denying rule to the *pambasileus*: "It remains only to obey (*peithesthai*) such a man and for him to be sovereign not by turns but simply" (1288a28–29). This seems a strong statement, but since *peithesthai* can mean equally "to obey" and "to be persuaded by," the ambiguity of Aristotle's treatment of kingship remains to the end. For a king to rule without consent may be good household management, but it is not political justice. For him to rule with consent may be political rule, but it is not kingship and therefore not what he deserves. It is not just.

Political life requires that the question of justice have been raised in the city; in this way, it begins in *aporia*. The general answer to the question of justice is equality: to give to each what he deserves. Any regime in which equals are treated unequally or unequals equally is a defective political order. In the end, however, this proves to mean that all regimes save one are defective, and this one, *pambasileia*, is not really a regime. All regimes are necessarily defective because their perfection would require putting together good rule with consent based on knowledge of one's true situation. With such knowledge, men would not need to be ruled; without it, they cannot give their consent. Political life aims at a good that it can therefore never achieve. It aims at a wealth or being (*ousia*) that is incompatible with awareness of what that being is. Awareness is not possible without some imperfection—some poverty, as Aristotle himself indicates in his account of why the rule of law is superior to the rule of men: "One, then, bidding the laws to rule, seems to bid god and mind alone to rule, while the one bidding a man to rule adds also a beast" (1287a28–30). But, as we saw, like all versions of pure mind, the law, by itself, has no motive to do anything. It can rule perfectly only because it does not wish to rule, and because it does not wish to rule, it cannot rule. Ultimately, political rule must be the rule of men.

If political life is to be both good and political, it must somehow combine the questioning and sense of need that is the defining feature of democracy with the substantial standards of justice for which oligarchy and, finally, *pambasileia* stand. Political life must combine seeking and having.[42] In general, philosophy is the model for this mixture; in particular, Book 3 itself is a model. By beginning with a democratic bias and concluding with a praise of absolute kingship, Book 3 reflects the fact that the common good cannot be defined except in terms of a virtue that forces us to think in terms of the ultimately uncommon good of the best man. Similarly, questioning makes no sense apart from the expectation of answers that, once attained, put an end to the activity giving rise to them. At the same time, the meaning of answers fades as their questions are forgotten. Philosophy is the perennial attempt to remember original questions so as to shed light on contemporary answers. Similarly, the discussion of kingship at the end of Book 3 never simply does away with the democratic *aporia* that gave rise to it.

There are various signs in Book 3 that we are meant to pay close attention to Aristotle's own activity in producing his account, his questioning, as well as to the content of the account, his answers. The most striking, we have already seen—the use of *aporia* to mean poverty politically on the level of Aristotle's account at the same time that it is used to mean something like question or puzzle philosophically on the level of Aristotle's and our activity. This pattern is repeated throughout Book 3. *Ison* means "equal" on the level of content of the argument; *isôs* means "perhaps" on the level of the narration (1282b14–25). In one sentence Aristotle refers to what is common, *to koinon*, for the citizens, and the common, *koinêi*, way of understanding citizens (1283b42–43). He makes a distinction between prior, *proteras*, and subsequent, *husteras*, regimes, the one being the good regimes and the other those deviating from them, and then in a parenthetical remark indicates that what he means will become clear later, *husteron* (1275a39–1279b4). Aristotle is funnier than is ordinarily recognized, but his playfulness is generally to some purpose. Here it forces us to recognize the necessity of thinking the account being given together with that of which it is the account. Does Aristotle's later "clearer" account of defective regimes derive from his earlier account as defective regimes derive from good regimes? Is his political philosophy then no less a second sailing than the cities he describes in his political philosophy?

Book 3 is political philosophy in the sense that terms used to describe political life reappear in different contexts to describe the movement of Aristotle's thought about political life. This occurs not only in these obvious cases but in countless less obvious ways. By calling it odd (*atopon*) that those in the banausic or vulgar class are neither citizens, metics nor foreigners (according to the account as of chapter 4), does not Aristotle wish us to recall his use of *topos* as place in the earlier discussion of what a city was, and does he not wish us to see that the real difficulty is that the vulgar are placeless (*atopos*)? And when he uses *theteon* to indicate what must be set down, does Aristotle mean what must be set down in his inquiry into the city or what must be set down in the city into which he is inquiring, or does he mean to collapse the difference between the two?[43]

The question, "What is the city?" is the being of the city, for political life is above all a conscious choice of a way of life—a regime. Like philosophy, the city begins in *aporia* and can never leave it behind, lest its way of life become simply mechanical and not self-aware; the city is what it calls itself. At the same time, the city is not simply what it calls itself, for it will always be constituted by a partial answer to the question it raises. And even this answer will gradually become a shadow of itself as the original question is forgotten. The city's understanding of justice will, therefore, tend to become a caricature of itself because the organizing principle of its regime will fall short of giving to each what he is due. Book 3 acknowledges the "obvious" way of overcoming this difficulty—awarding rule to those of extraordinary wisdom—in order to show that the obvious way is impossible. The best regime must be modeled on philosophy but for this very reason cannot be ruled by philosophers, whose own awareness of the regime would rob others of such awareness.

Politics and philosophy is the theme of the *Politics* as a whole. We saw that Book 1 is an account of the transformation of the unselfconscious natural community—the family—into the city, the nature of which is to be self-conscious; it reveals politics to be philosophical. And we saw that Book 2 shows how all understanding of the city takes place within the city and is therefore political; it reveals philosophy to be political. In Book 3, after demonstrating the kinship between philosophy and politics by spelling out the self-conscious nature of all political life as a combination of *aporia* and *ousia*, democracy and kingship, Aristotle shows this combination to be as inevitable as its perfection is impossible. The rest of the *Politics* divides in two. The being of the city is its self-understanding, but the city will never understand itself correctly. The city is essentially a self-misunderstanding. To understand the various defective regimes requires seeing the specific ways in which philosophy and politics combine problematically in them. This will be the concern of Books 4–6. It will then remain for Aristotle to show how the city at its best manages the *aporia* at its core. This will be the task of Books 7 and 8.

Part II

Politics

Chapter Four

The Soul of the *Polis*:
Politics Book 4

Since Book 4 begins something quite new in the *Politics*, its place in the whole is of some importance. There is an established scholarly dispute about the order of the books.[44] Book 4 contains several references (e.g., 1289a, 1290a, 1293b) to "earlier" passages in the *Politics* easily understood as references to Books 7 and 8. This, along with the fact that Book 7 begins with almost the same words that conclude Book 3, leads many editors to place Books 7–8 after Books 1–3 and conclude the *Politics* with Books 4–6, a radical change given that every apparent reference in Book 4 to Books 7–8 can be understood unproblematically as a reference to Book 3. In addition, Aristotle ends the *Nicomachean Ethics* with a sketch of the order of his inquiry into the *politeia* that, with the exception of Book 1, seems to correspond to the traditional order of the *Politics*. Finally, while the beginning of Book 7 is surely similar to the end of Book 3, the two passages are not identical. In fact, the differences are substantial. Barker, Lord, and Rackham construe the very last words of Book 3 as a sentence fragment. Others (Jowett and Sinclair) leave it out altogether.[45] However, it seems possible, if a little awkward, to translate it as part of the previous sentence, as follows:

> Having already defined these things, concerning the best *politeia*, we must try to say what way it comes to be by nature and how it is in fact necessary for the one intending to make an appropriate inquiry (*skepsin*) about it to establish it. (1288b3–8)

65

Aristotle would then end Book 3 by acknowledging the connection between investigating the best regime (philosophy) and instituting the best regime (politics), an issue that in general binds the whole of the *Politics* together and, in particular, connects Book 3 to Book 4. Book 7, on the other hand, begins as follows: "About the best *politeia*, it is necessary that the one intending to make an appropriate inquiry (*zêtêsin*) first define what is the most choiceworthy life" (1323a14–16). Not only are different words used for inquiry (*skepsis* and *zêtêsis*), but, even given the similarities of the passages, the word order is markedly different.[46] Far from being a sign that these two passages were originally the same, this seems to suggest that they were different, albeit perhaps with a similarity meant to be noticed.

That one can even consider reordering the books of the *Politics* is a sign of the curious extent to which the parts of the book are whole by themselves and can stand alone. Still, their order is not as arbitrary as it first seems. The first three books treat the city from the perspective of its perfection. They culminate in Book 3 in the problem of kingship, a problem that is really the same as the problem of political philosophy (1282b–1283a). The perfect city proves to be impossible because the best city is not a city; human life is at odds with the perfection of human life. Books 4–6, concerned with political life as necessarily defective, follow directly after the account of this "perfection." Accordingly, neither *philosophia* nor any word cognate with it occurs in these books. Books 7–8 are concerned with the extent to which the necessarily imperfect character of political life can be taken into account from within political life and so provide the principle for whatever perfection is available to men politically. They, therefore, follow naturally after Book 6.

As a whole in its own right, Book 4 seems most of all to be about the regime (*politeia*) called polity (*politeia*). Accordingly, it is about the form of *polis* that, presumably unlike all the other forms, is what it is. A member of a class bearing the name of the whole as its own might reasonably be expected to be in some way paradigmatic of the class.[47] Yet it is striking that unlike the cases of kingship, aristocracy, oligarchy, democracy, and even tyranny, it is not clear whether any *polis* has ever understood itself to be a polity. This is the underlying puzzle of Book 4. How do those who live in a polity understand the regime in which they live?

This question is connected to another already present in Book 3 concerning the relation between a good man and a good citizen. Even on the level of citizenship, goodness is equivocal. A city requires citizens who are at once good at ruling and good at being ruled. But being willing to accept what another says to do, if it is a virtue at all, is surely not the same virtue as knowing what to do oneself. If the good citizen were simply one perfect at being ruled and totally devoted to the common good, he would be disturbingly mechanical. His one-dimensional devotion to the common good would be altogether formal, for he would not really know what the common good is. The good man as ruler presumably would have more depth; his devotion to his city would include a concrete notion of what it might mean for citizens to fare well. Yet would this knowledge not require an attachment to some sphere other than the public? When a legislator formulates laws to improve the lot of those who live in his district, ought he not know, for example, whether these laws should attempt to encourage a certain sort of family life? His judgment as legislator is not altogether distinct from his judgment as child, parent, or sibling, businessman, doctor, or lawyer. In fact, the one depends on the others. Without the individual will, the general will is contentless because lives are ultimately lived not by cities but by human beings; the city is not an animal with its own goals and purposes. Accordingly, if the goal of a political order is that its citizens be happy, the public sphere is in some sense always answerable to the private. There can be no justice, no equitable distribution of goods, without an understanding of some good apart from equitable distribution. Were virtue solely justice, it would be nothing but empty goodwill, a will to do right without any notion of the content of right.[48] Suppose it should become necessary to sacrifice one's family in defense of one's city. This would not even be a sacrifice, let alone ennobling, unless one felt a powerful loyalty to the family. To be a genuinely good citizen thus requires a less than complete devotion to one's city. What, then, is the devotion characteristic of the good citizen in the best regime? And how would he understand the defining principle of the regime to which he is devoted?

In Book 4 Aristotle discusses the difference between a democracy of farmers and a democracy of artisans. As city dwellers, the artisans' attachment to their *polis* grows at the expense of the private sphere. Unlike farmers, who work at home, and for whom political participation is a luxury, artisans can go regularly to the assembly. Like contemporary commuters who travel daily from home to job, they become partially detached from their families. They are more like the individuals making up the *polis* in Book 3 than the members of a household making up the *polis* in Book 1. Farmers are not such pure citizens as are artisans, yet paradoxically, in their incomplete devotion to the public sphere, farmers make better citizens.[49] The question raised in Book 3 about the relation between the good man and the good citizen is thus answered in Book 4: In the good regime the good man is the same as the good citizen only if the good regime is by design not complete—not the "best." Political life is in principle defective; the good man will be a good citizen only if he lives in a regime that requires that he be incompletely devoted to it. The good man would then be incompletely devoted to any city in which he lived. The best city would demand this; lesser cities would deserve it. But what exactly does it mean to devote oneself fully to the principle of incomplete devotion?

That Book 4 is concerned with this question is not at once obvious. On the surface, it is an account of the variety of political regimes. Rationally specifying this variety would amount to a science of politics as it really is and would require saying something about political life other than describing the regime that is simply best. To vary from the best means to be less than the best. Now, a scientific account of this variety would have to describe it not as accidental, but as in some way governed by necessity. According to Aristotle, the transformation of one regime into another has a natural cause (1289b24–26). Book 4 therefore begins with a reflection on political science and why it must treat not only the best, but also the variety of regimes (1288b–1289b). Aristotle then discusses why variety is inevitable and why in particular oligarchy and democracy are inevitable (1289b–1291b). After specifying the varieties of democracy and oligarchy (1291b–1293a), polity and aristocracy (1293a–1294b) and tyranny (1295a), he returns to polity as that regime which is best for most cities (1295a–1296b)— that is, he discusses the virtues of the middle class—followed by a treatment of which regimes are advantageous for which cities (1296b–1297b). Book 4 concludes with an account of the political institutions—deliberative, judicial, and the arrangement of offices— characteristic of each type of regime.

The beginning of Book 4 is puzzling. No matter what one's position on the scholarly question of the order of the books of the

Politics, Book 4 must come somewhere after Book 3. But why should the nature of a science of politics become a question after the account of the variety of regimes in Book 3, and why should a reflection on science be the appropriate beginning for a discussion of defective political regimes? Is there a connection between the question of science and the question of politics? Let us turn to the first sentence.

> In all the arts and sciences that do not come to be with respect to a part but are complete (*teleiais*) concerning a single class (*genos*) it belongs to one [art or science] to contemplate what is appropriate concerning each class. . . . (1288b10–13)

Since each class is treated as a whole by only one science, when something seems to be treated by more than one science, at least one of them is not treating it as a whole. Sociology, political science and economics overlap. They are therefore either distinct in name only, or else only one or none of them treats the object of its inquiry as a whole. There seems a curious similarity between a scientific whole and a political whole—a regime or *politeia*. While any regime has parts, in claiming to be directed at a common good, it claims to treat these parts not separately but as parts of a whole. And the whole in terms of which it claims to treat them is itself in some sense comprehensive.[50] *Politikê* is comprehensive and authoritative.[51] Any regime must claim to know a comprehensive and authoritative good and thus tacitly claims a scientific understanding of itself from within. It claims to know the principle according to which it is a whole and according to which the importance of each of its parts is to be measured. We are political animals insofar as having *logos* enables us to articulate the useful and the harmful (1253a); justice and injustice are impossible without this awareness of good and evil. *Poleis* vary according to how they articulate the good and the bad to themselves—that is, according to their understandings of justice. These understandings are their *politeiai* and are spelled out in their laws. Fully to understand democratic justice, with its emphasis on equality, one would have to understand the claim to rule by right made by the part of the city called the *dêmos*. It would require that one understand the whole constituted with the *dêmos* as its head. Similarly, in oligarchy the rich do not claim to rule as a matter of superior strength but as a matter of right. They claim the whole is at its best when they are in control. This is the "scientific" claim every city must make. Every *polis* is what it is by virtue of its *politeia*; every *politeia* is a claim to have *politikê*, the knowledge or science of politics.

Nevertheless, the nature of *politikê* is ambiguous. It involves not only inspecting the single best regime but also whatever regime is possible given existing circumstances. Accordingly,

> [I]t is no less a deed to set a regime (*politeia*) straight than it is to establish it from the beginning, just as to unlearn one thing and learn another [is no less a deed] than to learn from the beginning. Hence, in addition to what has been said, the *politikos* [the one practiced in *politikê*] ought to be able to come to the aid of existing regimes as was also said before. (1289a4–8)

Knowing how to tinker with existing regimes involves a further ambiguity.

> So the differences among regimes ought not to be ignored, how many there are and in how many ways combined. And with this same prudence (*phronêsis*) [one ought] to look at the best laws and those suitable for each of the regimes. (1289a10–13)

The "same prudence" involves knowledge of the variety of regimes and knowledge of what is best for any particular existing regime. This seems sensible. To know the parts of a *polis* means to know their places within the larger whole, which, in turn, means to know what the regime would look like if the parts were out of place or disproportionately emphasized, or to know the various possible defective regimes. If this prudence is genuine, the one possessing it will also know the characteristic defect of his own regime, supposing that it is not perfect. The prudent man will thus only be fully patriotic in the perfect regime; elsewhere, his loyalty will be questionable. On the other hand, if he were altogether loyal, his prudence would be suspect, and his relative ignorance would be among the causes of the imperfection of his regime. Unlike the other arts and sciences to which Aristotle compares it, *politikê* gives itself its own ends—it provides its own hypothesis. Thus, to mistake the principle of the whole with respect to the *polis* not only leads to a misunderstanding of the variety of regimes; it is also what is responsible for generating this variety. The misunderstanding of what is best *is* the deviation from the best. *Politikê* seems to be a sci-

ence in which a mistake on the level of analysis, an eidetic mistake, has practical—genetic—consequences.[52] One who practices
gymnastikê forms certain conclusions about what makes the body
healthy and strong but does not thereby define what constitutes
health and strength. If his regimen is wrong, the error will show up
in the body in such a way that even he will recognize it. One claiming the prudence characteristic of *politikê*, however, should he err
democratically in his understanding of the *politeia*, would err not
only about the means to the health of the *polis* but also about the
nature of this health. While he could commit a discoverable error—
for example, failing to prescribe the correct cure for a collective ill
like unemployment—he might be quite pleased with the result of
his error. This is why Aristotle insists that "rebuilding a *politeia* is
no less a deed than producing [it] from the beginning" (1289a4–5).
The art (*technê*) of politics—constructing a *politeia*—is the same
as the science or knowledge (*epistêmê*) of politics, since to persuade
men of the benefits of a political order means to articulate it as a
form of regime.

Aristotle begins Book 4—the practical part of the *Politics*—by
reflecting on the nature of science and art because they share something fundamental with all actual political regimes. He begins this
discussion by dismissing in passing those sciences and arts having
come to be *kata morion*—with respect to a part (1288b10–12). Science must treat wholes—things complete in their own rights and
thus belonging by nature to a single inquiry. Yet we know very well
that something is always lost when we treat a part of the whole as
though it were altogether apart from the whole. *Gymnastikê* may
be the *technê* of living body, but, granted that one can treat
living body apart from soul, is not this independence purchased at
a price? A gymnastic trainer can ill afford to be unaware of the
various bodily effects—sometimes good, sometimes bad—that des-
perate desire to win can have on competitors. He too must keep
body and soul together. The sciences, then, are only artificially
whole; all art and science come to be *kata morion*—with respect to
a part. Like politics, science and art necessarily treat parts as though
they were wholes. But this is just to treat the names that we give
things as though they completely exhausted the beings of the things
they name.[53] This principle assures the incompleteness of all the
partial sciences. At some point gymnastic will either have to acknowledge its partiality or blindly treat bodies as though they were

as separable from souls in deed as they are in speech. By compar-
ing politics and science with respect to the wholes with which they
deal, Aristotle suggests that the imperfection of political life might
be the same as the imperfection of science. Just as being truly "scientific" might ultimately mean understanding the partiality of each
of the sciences, being truly "political" might ultimately mean understanding the partiality of each of the various regimes. Politics
would then be something like a science of science (and Socrates
would be the only one in Athens who practiced the true political
art), although this higher-order science would be different in kind
from the others. As knowledge of the incompleteness of the sciences, it would be something like knowledge of ignorance; it would be
philosophy.[54] The particular sciences would then stand to philosophy as the defective regimes of Books 4–6 stand to the "best" regime of Book 7.

Books 1–3 of the *Politics* make clear that, while political life
cannot exist without a self-conscious understanding of what is good,
there is nevertheless always a tension between the deeds of a *polis*
and its self-understanding. There is always a misperception of the
end of the *polis* from within the *polis*. Book 4 is constructed with
this problem in mind. The various *politeiai* are like the various
sciences, each presupposing and not calling into question its own
wholeness. Insofar as each is really only partial, this assertion of
wholeness renders each defective. All "sciences" save the one that
is comprehensive and architectonic are necessarily partial and so
necessarily defective; elsewhere, Aristotle calls such a nondefective
science both first philosophy, or theology, and *politikê*.[55] Its status
as knowledge or *epistêmê* is by no means obvious. In the *Metaphysics*, for example, Aristotle repeatedly characterizes the ultimate
concern of first philosophy as the *ti esti* or "What is it?" of a thing.
That the subject-matter of metaphysics is a question makes it look
suspiciously like knowledge of ignorance.[56] And in the *Nicomachean
Ethics*, just after arguing that the concern of *politikê* is the single
human good, Aristotle describes it as the science of the beautiful and the just, two things repeatedly in tension throughout the
book as a whole.[57] If the science of politics treats something only
problematically whole, then it too begins to look like knowledge of ignorance. Ordinarily, the particular *epistêmai* and *politeiai*, in mistaking their own wholeness, misunderstand themselves.
If misunderstanding is the principle of all *politeiai* (regimes), the
question remains what it would mean for a *politeia* (polity) to be

good, for it would have to make misunderstanding the principle of good politics.

Having asserted the theoretical status of knowledge of what is defective (1288b35–40), Aristotle seems poised to consider the whole range of defective *politeiai*. Strangely, however, this is not what he does. He first identifies the *politeia* with an order concerning offices, how they are distributed, what is sovereign in the *politeia*, and what the end of the community is (1289a15–18). There are various species (*eidê*) of *politeiai* and so a variety of legitimate communities. Accordingly, there is also a variety of legitimate ends. What, then, will this variety include?

> And since in the first inquiry concerning regimes (*politeiai*) we distinguished three right regimes (*politeiai*)—kingship, aristocracy, and polity (*politeia*)—and three falling short of these—tyranny of kingship, oligarchy of aristocracy, and democracy of polity—and aristocracy and kingship have been spoken about (for to look at the best regime is the same as to speak about these terms). . . . (1289a26–33)

Aristotle began Book 4 with a description of political science—*politikê*. He now asserts that kingship and aristocracy were previously treated.[58] Does this mean that they are not included in political science, perhaps that they are not genuine political alternatives? Aristotle will discuss tyranny later in Book 4 (1295a1–24), but the account seems pro forma.[59] The real variety of regimes seems to have shrunk to three—democracy, oligarchy, and polity. The shrinkage does not stop here, since the various species of democracy are defined by the modifications by which they temper the extreme form—the tyrannical and lawless rule of the majority (1291b29–1292a38)—and the various species of oligarchy are said to be modifications of dynastic rule without law (1292a39–b10). As the modifications of pure democracy tend to be oligarchic and of pure oligarchy, democratic, in a certain sense all regimes (*politeiai*) are polities (*politeiai*); democracy and oligarchy are simply the extreme versions of polity. Book 4, then, concentrates on democracy and oligarchy because all regimes are really perversions of polity.

Tyranny is the worst such perversion.

> For it is necessary for the falling away from the first and most divine to be worst, and kingship necessarily has either the name alone, not

being such, or being so through the great superiority of the one ruling as king. (1289a39–1289b2)

The best kind is finally superior even to the law (1287a4–5). The best thus depends solely on its being best in order to be best. It contains no institutions to prevent it from turning bad. But no less than tyranny, oligarchy, and democracy, kingship and presumably aristocracy (which is similarly opposed to the second worst regime, oligarchy) are characterized by the absence of law—the *polis'* pre-scription to itself of the best way to live: "For laws ought to be set down, and all set them down, with a view to the regimes" (1289a13–14). Law is the self-awareness of the *polis*. All regimes, to be re-gimes, must be self-aware. At the same time, the "best regimes" seem not to be self-aware. One can imagine the all-powerful king of Book 3 ruling in silence; his subjects would need have no thought other than the most general sense that they were being ruled by the best for the best. This is why polity (*politeia*) is such an important form of regime (*politeia*) for Aristotle; it bears the name of the class because it exemplifies the contradiction essential to the being of the class. A polity must be self-aware, and yet, because all existing regimes seem to be defective forms of polity, no *politeia* is really a *politeia*. In order to be what it is a polity must know itself to be what it is not. In this sense, the defining feature of *politeiai* is that they perceive themselves wrongly. But why?

Democracy and oligarchy may be understood as deviant forms of polity, but "polity, to speak simply, is a mixture of oligarchy and democracy" (1293b34–35).[60] In Book 4 we move in our understand-ing from parts that do not really exist (democracy and oligarchy) to a whole that may never have arisen (polity: 1296a36–37), while at the same time we are moving from whole to parts. The book begins with the question of the relation of whole to part in its con-nection with science. Science requires treating the object of one's inquiry with respect to the whole of which it is a part. However, whole and part are treated ambiguously throughout the book.

The cause, then, of the multitude of regimes is that of every city there is a numerical multitude of parts. For first we see all cities being composed of households, and then again of this multitude some are necessarily well-off (*euporous*), some poor (*aporous*) and some middling (*mesous*), and of those well-off and those poor, there are the armed and the unarmed. (1289b27–34)

At the same time,

> That there are a multitude of regimes and what the cause is has been
> said. But let us say why there are more than have been said,
> and what they are and on account of what, taking our beginning from
> the things said earlier. For we agree that every city has not one
> part but several. Then, just as if we intended to grasp species of
> animal, we would first divide off what it is necessary for every an-
> imal to have—for example, some of the organs of perception, some-
> thing for working on and, receiving food such as a mouth and a
> stomach, and, in addition to these, parts by which each is moved—
> and if there were only so many but of these there were different
> ones—I mean, for example, a number of kinds of mouth, of stom-
> ach and of the organs of perception, and further also of the parts
> for movement—the number of the variety of yokings of these things
> of necessity would make a number of classes of animals. For it
> is not possible for the same animal to have a multitude of differences
> of mouth or similarly of ears, so that when all the possible com-
> binations of these are taken, they will make the species of animal,
> and there will be as many species of animal as there are yokings
> of parts and in the same way also of the aforementioned regimes.
> (1290b21–39)

The city is made up of parts, but in one case the parts are given
before the whole, and in the other the whole determines the number and nature of the parts. In the first case the movement is from
known parts to an unknown whole and all parts are treated equally.
In the second case the movement is from the demands of a whole,
an animal, to the parts minimally necessary for the existence of the
whole. These parts are essentially functions; in no way prior to the
whole they constitute, they are rather defined by its needs. So, for
example, Aristotle can speak of the parts necessary for the movement of the animal without ever indicating their number or shape
or whether they are responsible for movement on land, in water,
through the air, or in thought.

The variety of regimes is inevitable given the division of any
city into a multitude of parts. Because the parts are not simply arbitrary but reflect the various functions necessary for collective life
(for example, every community must make provisions for rearing
children, raising food, producing artifacts, and defending itself), the
variety of regimes is classifiable. It is subject to a science. On the
other hand, any regime will be imperfect owing to the accidental
way in which various functions get combined in one human being.

The parts of any city must include fathers and farmers. It is an accident, although no less generally the rule, that these two functions will be combined in one person. The very best *polis* would presumably have the best farmers and the best fathers, but what necessity requires that the two be compatible, or, if they are, then what about being a father and at the same time being an artisan or a soldier? Is excellence in raising children indifferent to whether a father lives and works at home or is away from home for long periods of time? And are soldiers better or worse when they have children to whom they are attached?

The perfect political order, the "true city," would seem to require either that each citizen perform one and only one function—one man, one art—or that the multiple functions in the same citizen fit so perfectly with one another that they in effect constitute a more comprehensive function.[61] The natural complexity of human beings is what forces this difficulty. We do not make very perfect parts for, at the very least, our performance of any task will always have a double motive—to do the job well and to benefit ourselves. An adequate analysis of the *polis* is, therefore, impossible on the basis of an abstract classification of needs, since the parts of the *polis* are not univocal in their use but are beings with multiple functions. This is only to say that no pure analysis of the *polis* is possible. The parts of the *polis*, which in some way must be understood to be equal, are not its *eidê*. They cannot be treated democratically, as though all were equally necessary and could be placed together with no governing order.[62] Every citizen must not only perform the function of his art but also consider his own good; each art will always be accompanied by the "money-making art." This issue, of course, figures prominently in Plato's *Republic* where the principle of one man-one art founders, either because artisans will be governed both by the rules constituting their arts and by the need to make a profit, or because those particularly suited to rule, the philosophers, practice an "art" that has nothing to do with rule, and so the fortuitous combination of philosophy and kingship violates the founding principle of the regime.[63]

Aristotle's first enumeration of the variety of regimes (Book 3, 1279a22–b10) was based on two principles—the form (*eidos*) of rule (rule of one, few, or many) and whether rule was directed at the good. These two principles show themselves in individuals as the double meaning of citizenship; we are at once equal participants and heterogeneous parts of the *polis*. Aristotle comments on this accidental, but fundamental, feature of political life in a curious way.

> It is apparent then that there are a multitude of regimes differing from one another in form (*eidos*), for these parts differ from themselves in form. For the order of offices (*arkhai*) is a regime, and all distribute this either according to the power (*dunamis*: ability) of those participating or according to some equality shared by them—I mean such as by the poor, or the well-off or something shared by both as a pair. There are necessarily then just as many regimes as there are orders reflecting the superiorities and differences of the parts. But there seem to be two especially, just as with the winds some are said to be northern, some southern, and the others deviations (*parekbaseis*)[64] from these, so also of regimes two [are said to be], the *dêmos* and oligarchy. For they make aristocracy a form of oligarchy as being a rule of the few [olig-archy], and so-called polity (*politeia*) [they make] rule of the *dêmos* [demo-cracy], just as among the winds [they make] the western [a form] of the northern and the eastern of the southern. (1290a6–20)

At first glance, it looks accidental that the various winds get described in terms of the northern and the southern, but Aristotle goes on to compare the north wind to the Dorian mode in music and the south wind to the Phrygian. The first—warlike, tense, and like the rule of a master—is likened to oligarchy; the second—peaceful, relaxed, and soft—is called demotic (1290a21–29).[65] This sort of division seems to hold true as well of the winds, the northern being more frequently responsible for harsh weather and the southern for mild weather. What seems at first an accidental contraction of the variety of winds thus proves on reflection to reveal a principle. The eidetic classification of regimes, like the classification of winds and musical harmonies, gives way to a classification based on the pleasant and the harsh. Oligarchy and democracy take center stage in Book 4 because the principle differentiating them overpowers the eidetic classification of regimes rooted in the various possible combination of parts. The crucial political distinction is between the pleasant and the harsh. It more or less corresponds to the distinction between citizen as heterogeneous part performing a function in a larger whole and citizen as homogeneous part sharing in the regime by dint of being equal to all other citizens. Citizens are simultaneously means to some further end and ends in themselves, have duties and rights, and contribute to and receive from the *po-*

lis; the first of each pair is harsh, the second pleasant. This distinction is at the root of the primacy of oligarchy and democracy in
Book 4.

The political problem is how to combine citizens as parts, spe-
cialized tools, with citizens as wholes, ends in themselves. The problem first emerges because as wholes we are repositories of more
than one power or ability, but like all multipurpose tools, we are
not very efficient. That we are comprehensive means that we are
not precise. Aristotle indicates the depth of this problem in a curious way. Having discussed the variety of *eidê* of animal in terms
of the possible combinations of its parts understood in terms of the
functions necessary for its existence, he enumerates the compara-
ble parts of the *polis*:

1. those dealing with food—farmers
2. the vulgar or mechanical class
3. the marketing or commercial class
4. hired laborers
5. warriors

Here follows a digression on the "true city" of Plato's *Republic*.
When the list continues, Aristotle seems to have skipped something.

7. those performing public works with their property—the
    well-off
8. the demiurgic class that performs public works by holding
    office

The most obvious difficulty is that Aristotle jumps from the fifth
member of his list to the seventh. But perhaps we are meant to
understand the fifth, the warriors, to be dual in its very nature. Then
it would be in some way both fifth and sixth on the list. Warriors
are introduced not to constitute the city, but to defend what has been
already constituted. Without warriors, the city will be defenseless
against attack and consequently "worth being called a slave by nature" (1291a9), but a *polis* is necessarily self-sufficient (*autarkês*)
and cannot be slavish. "This has been said in the *Republic* (*politeia*) wittily but not adequately" (1291a11–12) because in the *Republic* the military class is introduced as an afterthought, as though it
could be added to the other classes of citizen—weaver, farmer, shoe-
maker, and builder are the initial four—after "the city of necessi-

ty" or the "true city" or the "city of sows" has already been established. It may be that only when the city as a whole is threatened does the need for a warrior class become clear, but only when the city becomes aware of itself *as a whole* does it become a city. No city exists, properly speaking, prior to the existence of the warrior class because a city needs a part within it that is aware of it as a whole. Warriors are the first sign of this self-consciousness since to do their job they must distinguish between friend and enemy, outsider and insider. It is thus no accident that Aristotle's digression from the warrior class leads first to a comment on the inadequacy of Socrates' "true city" in *Republic* Book 2 and then to a reflection on that "part" of the city that judges and deliberates.[66]

> But even among the four (or however many who share) it is necessary for there to be someone who metes out and judges what is just. If then someone were to posit soul of animal as more of a part than body, then such things of cities as the military, the [part] participating in the adjudication of justice, and in addition to these the deliberating [part], which are the function of political understanding, must be posited as more [a part] than those contributing to necessary need. (1291a22–28)

One part of the *polis* is like the soul of an animal, but it is hard to separate from the other parts. Accordingly, Aristotle mentions it rather prominently and links it first with the warrior part and then with the judging and deliberating parts, but leaves it out of his official enumeration. The unnumbered sixth item on Aristotle's list of the city's parts is its soul—the only part that is, properly speaking, political (1291a41–b2), which, for this very reason, does not count as a part of the *polis*.

The soul is the principle of motion in animals.[67] Aristotle began his enumeration of the parts of the *polis* by likening it to an animal, but of course the *polis* is not really alive. It cannot really move; insofar as it appears to move it is moved by one or more of its living parts—its citizens. We are so accustomed to using a certain shorthand that it is easy to forget that government agencies, strictly speaking, do not do anything; all political motion is initiated by human beings. The city's "soul" may be its most important and only truly political "part," but to be at all, it must be lodged in one of the lesser, really existing parts. The problem becomes especially clear in the warrior class. Either the military are the people so that, for example, farmers bear arms (1291a30–31), or they are a separate class. In the first case, the military will be distorted by the idiosyncrasies of the part in which they are lodged (farmer-soldiers in Washington's army during the American Revolution are said to have been notorious for deserting at harvest time). In the second case, the military become utterly detached from the people and soon come to think of themselves as the real city, now master, and no longer servant. But the military is the first sign of the city's self-consciousness, its soul, which is either utterly detached from the city, and so, while perhaps pure, not the soul of the *city*, or lodged in a part and therefore necessarily affected by the accidental characteristics of this part. To be, the city must have a soul—a *politeia*. What a *politeia* means, however, is that some part of a *polis* mistakenly understands itself as the whole.

Because the most significant of the parts into which the city divides are the rich and the poor, the fundamental political alternative will be to lodge the soul of the city either in one or the other or, to use Aristotle's favorite word, "somehow" in both. This, their union, can be understood to constitute polity. Yet

> it is impossible for the same men to be poor and rich. Hence these especially seem to be parts of the *polis*, the well-off (*euporoi*) and the needy (*aporoi*). (1291b5–8)

Rich and poor are not accidentally parts, for they cannot be combined. The question is not so much what each has, since what constitutes poverty and wealth will vary considerably from regime to regime, but what each thinks. Perceiving oneself as poor is at odds with perceiving oneself as rich. The poor (*aporoi*) seem to themselves to be without means (a-poros); the rich (*euporoi*) seem to themselves to be well provided with means (eu-poros). Because one cannot easily think of one's way as simultaneously thwarted and advanced, it is hard to imagine a good that could be perceived as common to both poor and rich, although it is perhaps not impossible (philosophy, in particular, comes to mind as a strange togetherness of *aporia*—poverty or perplexity—and *ousia*—property or being).[68]

Democracy is based on a perceived equality of need. Accordingly, the democratic vice is envy (1295b23), and democratic crimes are born of need (the way to cure crime is to alleviate poverty). Oligarchy, on the other hand, is based on a perceived superiority, wealth. Its characteristic vice is condescension (1295b24), and oligarchic crimes are born of hybris (the way to cure crime is punishment). Democracy is essentially negatively determined. Human beings, once defined as needy, need a positive articulation of their principle of community. Democracies are therefore particularly prone to flattery, demagoguery, and imperialism (1292a13–33). Oligarchy, on the other hand, breeds a certain inhumanity. What is initially a political distinction based on who has more wealth ends as a claim about who ought to have more wealth; oligarchy becomes hereditary (1292b5–10, 1293a28–31). Both of these principles ultimately destroy the common good and with it the city. Shared need is not sufficiently good, and a sense of superiority is not sufficiently shared.

Aristotle's solution is to mix the oligarchic and the democratic in polity—*politeia*.

> Now we have to show something about polity, for its power is more manifest now that we have defined the things concerned with oligarchies and democracies. For, to speak simply, polity is a mixture of oligarchy and democracy, but it is customary to call those tending toward democracy polities and those toward oligarchy rather aristocracies. . . . (1293b32–37)

But, given the immiscibility of *aporia* and *euporia*, how is this possible? It is noteworthy that Aristotle refers to "what is named polity" (1293b22) or "so-called polity" (1294a31); he also makes clear that such a regime may never have come to be or rarely (*oligakis*) and among few (*oligois*) (1296a36–38). Furthermore, when Aristotle says that "what we now call polities those before us called democracies" (1297b25–26), what does he mean by "we"? Do those living in polities call them polities, or is this simply what Aristotle calls them?[69] Does polity ever show itself as a mixture of democracy and oligarchy?

> This is the way of the mixture, for the mark of the good mixing of democracy and oligarchy is when it is possible to say that the same regime (*politeia*) is a democracy and an oligarchy. (1294b13–16)

> And in a beautifully mixed polity (*politeia*), it is necessary to seem both and neither. . . . (1294b35–36)

The mixture is thus successful if one can say that the regime is both oligarchy and democracy. Polity is characterized by a double seeming. Does this mean that it seems double to everyone, or that to those who want democracy, it seems democratic, to those who want oligarchy, oligarchic?

Polity (*politeia*) takes the necessarily mixed quality of every regime (*politeia*), as well as the necessary self-misunderstanding present in every regime, and makes these its principles. Accordingly, of the species of regime it alone bears the name of the genus. For this reason, however, its character as a compromise will never become clear to those who live in it. In distinguishing polity from aristocracy (1293a35–b22), Aristotle makes it clear that aristocracy is also a mixed regime. The very best regime looks to those who are best in point of virtue to be its rulers, but regimes in which rulers are chosen not only because of being best but also because of wealth are also aristocratic, as are regimes that look to wealth, virtue, and the *dêmos* (e.g., Carthage) and those that look to virtue and the *dêmos* (e.g., Sparta). Polity, in looking only to wealth and to the *dêmos*, is a regime in which there is no self-conscious choice of what is best. For this reason, its citizens tend to think of it as something else. Having finished his discussion of aristocracy in chapter 7, Aristotle begins chapter 8 by saying he will now discuss what is named polity. That he ends up returning to aristocracy is not accidental. The very nature of polity, not unlike philosophy, is that a discussion of it should turn into a discussion of something else.[70] Aristocracy presents itself as the rule of virtue. Oligarchy, when it does not present itself as aristocracy (1293b38–41), appeals to wealth as its principle. Democracy presents itself as the rule of the free. But to make the case for polity proves to require praise of mediocrity; it is a hard and uninspiring case to argue.

The key to polity is the middle class, and its status is problematic.

If it was said beautifully in the *Ethics* that the happy life is the unimpeded life according to virtue, and that virtue is a mean, it is necessary for the middle life to be best, the mean being possible to attain for each. And these same markers also belong to the virtues and vices of a city and of a regime for the regime is a certain life of a city. In all cities there are in fact three parts of the city—those very well-off, those very poor, and the third, those in the middle of these. Since, then, it is agreed that the moderate and the middle is best, it is apparent that even of the goods of fortune a middling possession is best of all. For it most easily obeys reason, but for one *over*beautiful, *over*strong, *over*ly well-born, or *over*rich, or the opposites of these, *over*beggarly, *over*weak, or *very* dishonored, it is hard to follow reason [italics are mine]. For some come rather to be hybristic and base in a big way, while others are scoundrels and do evil in a very little way. And acts of injustice come to be, on the one hand, on account of hybris and, on the other, on account of being a scoundrel. And further these [those in the middle] are least inclined to avoid ruling or to be eager to rule, and both of these are harmful to cities. (1295a36–b14)

In this account of polity, Aristotle makes an explicit appeal to his understanding of virtue in the *Nicomachean Ethics.* Virtue is a mean between two extremes; courage, for example, is the proper amount of fear and confidence, avoiding either too much fear and too little confidence (cowardice) or too much confidence and too little fear (rashness). Yet Aristotle also makes it clear (*Nicomachean Ethics* 1107a7–8, 1108b11–15) that the virtuous mean is itself an extreme because it is opposed qualitatively to each of the extremes. This is not really true of the middle class of a polity, which, therefore, has really not much to do with virtue. This class is only extreme in its avoidance of all extremes. As Aristotle describes them, those in the middle class do not aim at the mean as a peak of perfection; rather, they occupy a middle position because they do not want anything very much. Their "virtue" is the wholly negative one of successfully avoiding the string of "over's" that characterizes the extremes. They are the tepid class, solid and safe because unimaginative and unambitious. They are able to rule, but, because they do not long to rule, they are also capable of being ruled. Aristotle's polity is desirable primarily for its stability, but it purchases stability at the cost of encouraging mediocrity. Because its prime citizens do not seem to long for something other than political life, they do not want to make much of anything of political life. They, therefore, define the purpose of their regime as stable political life. The goal of this *politeia* is *politeia* and nothing other; its good is simply itself.

Book 4 began by identifying the primary subject-matter of the science of politics as the study of the best regime, the regime one would pray for above all (1288b21–23). Is mediocrity, however useful, ever something one would pray for? Aristotle repeatedly alludes to the possibility that polity is only "so-called" polity because no regime thinks of itself as a polity for very long. The problem might be put in the following admittedly non-Aristotelian way.

Book 4 is about the role of ideology in political life. The best regime in practice will be, like Sparta, an oligarchy with democratic
principles—an oligarchy that misunderstands itself as a democracy.
Or it will be a democracy that misunderstands itself as an oligarchy. In either case, the best regime will be a polity not in spite of,
but because, it does not know what it is. To hold anything high it
must not embrace its opposite, yet it requires the stabilizing
effect of opposition to what it holds high. It must therefore be
blind to the presence of this opposition. Political stability is
built on this sort of misunderstanding. However, stability has its
price. It is built either on mediocrity, ignorance, or both, and, in
its own way, it introduces a principle of instability. Since no polity
can ever live up to its articulated principle and, since this exemplifies what is true of all *politeiai*, every regime will of necessity contain within it the conditions for its own overthrow. It is
not accidental that Book 4 on polity is followed by Book 5 on
revolution.

Aristotle concludes Book 4 with an account of the different political institutions that support democracies, oligarchies, and polities, dividing the functions of the political "part" of any regime into
deliberative (the part that decides what will be done), officers, rulers or magistrates (the part that does what is decided), and judges
(the part that determines what has been done).[71] This triple account
of the soul of the *polis* makes clear that, apart from the earlier issue of whether the soul must be lodged in a part of the city so
that, for example, the assembly will be made up of farmers, the
political functions themselves overlap. In structure, the soul of the
polis is three; eidetically it must be understood to deliberate, rule,
and judge. In reality, however, these functions overlap and, in the
most extreme cases, tend to overlap completely. In extreme democracy, everyone decides, does, and judges everything, and, similarly,
in extreme oligarchy, a designated few do all of these things. In
both cases, the result is essentially nonpolitical because it obscures
the partiality of the political. The *polis* really seems to have a soul.
Only if some are concerned with some things and others with others is the distinction preserved between what concerns the city as a
whole and what concerns its particular parts. War, audits, and laws
concern it as a whole; particular court cases concern its parts. When
all deliberation concerns the whole—that is, when everything is
political—nothing is political; this is the extreme of democracy.
When no deliberation concerns the whole, then nothing is political;

this is the extreme of oligarchy. Political life requires that the city be aware of itself as a whole with parts. This becomes clear first in the distinction between the soul of the city—its self-aware "part"—and its other parts, those performing the necessary functions. But it turns out to be true even on the level of the soul itself. The self-aware part itself has parts; its structure is at odds with its nature. It is only problematically whole. The political institutions Aristotle treats are, therefore, replete with examples where the whole seems to be acting but serially, in such a way as to act by parts. Deliberation may be the job of all, but regimes will vary considerably according to whether all always deliberate or they do so in turn in smaller groups and about specified issues. Similarly, magistrates may be chosen by all at once or by a series of smaller groups where family, wealth, and reputation will have greater effect. In these and other ways, polities appear to act as a whole and therefore to avoid the anti-egalitarian principle necessarily present in any selection of a smaller governing group while actually introducing an oligarchic element into the regime.

Aristotle ends Book 4 as he began it, with a reflection on the problematic relation between part and whole in the *polis*. The city may be a whole that is aware of itself as having parts, but this awareness must always be lodged in a part and so can never be an accurate understanding of the whole. Furthermore, it is itself only problematically whole, since the principle of its wholeness must be lodged in a "part" of itself. The wholeness of the city is finally no less problematic than the wholeness of the beings who are its parts. It should come as no surprise then that, even when properly mixed, a regime will fail to understand itself correctly. Book 4 means to articulate the principle underlying the defectiveness of all political regimes—self-ignorance. Polity is paradigmatic because it acknowledges this principle in its being, its double seeming. This makes it not so much best to live in (although in some sense it is—i.e., in terms of stability) as best for illustrating the nature of political life as rooted in opinion, which is to say, false opinion. Were a *politeia* to know itself correctly, it would know that it does not know; it would have knowledge of ignorance. Aristotle leaves the discussion of this alternative to Books 7 and 8, but its possibility is the unifying theme of the entire *Politics*—the uncanny parallel between philosophy and political life.

Chapter Five

Erôs and Physics: *Politics* Book 5

Aristotle deals very little with kingship and tyranny in Book 4. They are the regimes without self-awareness—the cities without talk. Kingship doesn't need it, and tyranny doesn't allow it.[72] Both regimes lack a "loyal opposition" and hence are prone to extremes. Both rule without law, the means by which a city talks to itself about what it holds important. The possibility of regimes without self-awareness causes us to ask about those that are self-aware. Democracy and oligarchy exist mainly as objects of thought. While wealth and poverty certainly have an objective foundation, politically they are essentially comparative. To feel wealthy means to wish to preserve what one has; to feel poor means to want more. Accordingly, Aristotle's division of crimes—the breaking of laws—in Book 4 into those committed from need and those committed from hybris points to the fundamental character of democracy and oligarchy.[73] The problem most obvious in democracy is that its principle of unity is only negative and needs a positive articulation. While less evidently so, the principle of oligarchy is also negative. Democracy is a partnership based on mutual need. Oligarchy seems based on shared contempt of those who are not the "few," but since these few are defined by not being poor, hybris is simply a complicated reaction to one's neediness.[74] In general, then, the *polis* seems to be negatively determined; it is born of a mutual sense of need but without a sense of what precisely is needed. In Book 4, the heart of the most stable regime, polity, is a middle class that does not need anything very much. This does minimize strife in the city but, at the same time, also minimizes the city's sense of its own whole-ness, the strong sense of need that binds it together. Perfect polity is not possible because there can be no "ideology" of polity; inso-far as the regime becomes more deserving of support, it arouses less passionate support. This problem at the heart of all regimes is the subject of Book 5—*metabolê*, revolution or change.[75]

Aristotle's account is, predictably, well organized. He begins with the general causes of *metabolê* from one kind of regime into an-other (1301a–1304b). He then turns to the causes of revolution in four of his six basic forms of regime: democracy, oligarchy, aris-tocracy, and polity (1304b–1307b). In the third section, he deals with the manner in which regimes in general can be preserved from rev-olution (1307b–1310a). He then turns to a discussion of the remain-ing two forms of regime—monarchy and tyranny (1310a–1316a). It looks as though Aristotle is about to conclude Book 5 with an ac-count of how best to preserve tyranny, when he adds a brief attack on the treatment of the cause of the degeneration of regimes in Plato's *Republic* (1316a–b).

One may be committed in theory to the view that any argument of Aristotle's will reward serious study; in practice Book 5 proves a severe test of this principle. It seems boring, which is not to say that much of it does not seem true. Aristotle tries our patience with a list of changes from one kind of regime into another—aristocracy to democracy, polity to democracy, oligarchy to polity, aristocracy to oligarchy, oligarchy to democracy, democracy to oligarchy, oligarchy to aristocracy, polity to oligarchy, democracy to polity, democracy to aristocracy (notice that there is no account of the change from polity to aristocracy or vice versa)—as well as lists of the causes of political change—gain, fear, negligence, petti-ness, disproportionate growth of a part, contempt, preeminence, honor, hybris. These seem at first little more than unrelated collec-tions. Only when one notices how peculiar certain features of his account are does one begin to get a sense of Aristotle's real inten-tion in Book 5.

The book is queer in a variety of ways. Aristotle begins with the claim that the primary cause of political change is the percep-tion of injustice—not the fact, but the sense of whether one has been treated justly. This is interesting because it is simply the re-verse side of what Aristotle has previously argued (for example, in

Book 3) to be the fundamental principle underlying all regimes. All regimes are put together in terms of some dominant view of justice. Democracies understand justice to be equal treatment of all in all things. Oligarchies understand justice to be the proportionally unequal treatment of unequals. Both are right in their way. Men are equal in many respects and unequal in others. Democracies, however, characteristically err in thinking that equality in some respects justifies equality of treatment in all. Oligarchies err in thinking that inequality in wealth justifies unequal treatment with regard to everything. Perceiving it unjust that the rich are honored more than those who are equally good but poor builds resentment against the rich and prepares the way for revolution. Aristotle, in his equanimity, also makes it clear that oligarchs, perceiving themselves slighted if treated as though their greater monetary contribution to the *polis* deserved no more honor than the contribution of the poorest man, will be inclined to rebel out of a sense of wounded pride. Gain and hybris are at the top of each of Aristotle's lists of the causes of revolution. In both democracy and oligarchy, the underlying bias of the regime, which makes it what it is, also ensures that the possibility of perceived injustice is always present. It therefore ensures the possibility of revolution.

Thus far, all of this is perfectly straightforward. All regimes have imperfections; their imperfections provide the ground for dissatisfaction and so, in more extreme cases, for revolution. It is in the examples of this perception of injustice that Book 5 gets peculiar.

> Internal factions (*staseis*) arise, then, not about small things but from small things, but they are fought about great things. But even the small ones are especially strong when they arise among those who are sovereign, such as happened even in Syracuse in ancient times. For the regime changed as a result of the quarrels (*stasiasantôn*), concerning an erotic cause, of two young men belonging to those in power. For, while one was away, the other, although his comrade, won over by intrigue the beloved boy of the first, who then, in his anger seduced the other's wife into coming away with him. As a result, enlisting the citizen body, they divided everyone into factions. (1303b17–26)

Aristotle goes on to mention a groom who jilted his bride, whose relatives then retaliated and killed the groom; a father who went to war because he could not arrange a match between his sons and a wealthy man's daughters; a dispute over the marriage of an heiress, which led to the sacred wars in Phocis; and finally the following example:

> And also at Epidamnus the regime underwent revolution (*metebale*) because of marriage matters. For after one man had betrothed his daughter, the father of the one to whom she was betrothed, having just become one of the magistrates, fined him. The latter, being insulted, allied himself with those excluded from the regime. (1304a10–17)

In these examples Aristotle presents revolution as caused by the anger resulting from alliances that fail for reasons having to do with sexuality and frustrated sexuality. It all reads a bit like an afternoon soap opera.

What is somewhat peculiar in this section on the general causes of revolution is almost perversely peculiar in the treatment of tyranny at the end of Book 5. This section of the *Politics* is troubling. After presenting the causes of revolution in tyrannical regimes, Aristotle goes on to give an account, sometimes rather Machiavellian, of how tyrants ought to behave to avoid revolutions. Now, Aristotle partly redeems himself by suggesting that no tyranny lasts very long anyway. He then makes it clear that the surest way for a tyrant to preserve his rule is to appear just, and, of course, the appearance of justice is not so easy to distinguish from justice if you are on the receiving end. Still, all of this does not appear to justify Aristotle's long and detailed list of tyrants and their outrages, mostly sexual. We are given examples of rape, pederasty, insincere pederasty, pederasty in which the beloved is insulted by being asked playfully why he is not yet with child, wife-stealing, and castration—to mention only a few. So uncharacteristic of Aristotle is this lurid account that one translator, Sir Ernest Barker, for the only time in his entire edition, relegates an undisputed portion of the text of the *Politics* to a footnote. His reasons are worth relating.

> The translator has omitted these passages in the text. They are matters of scandal, or at best curiosities of history such as Aristotle with his encyclopedic habit loved to collect, rather than matters of politics and theory.[76]

Now, it is to be taken as a certain sign that something interesting is going on when an Oxbridge don's sense of propriety is offended.

What is most peculiar about Aristotle's account of revolution is the connection he tacitly makes between sex and violence. Sexual outrages seem to be the paradigm for that hybris which

> although having many parts, each of them is the cause of anger, and being angry, most men ordinarily attack for the sake of revenge and not preeminence. (1311a33–36)

Why there is so much emphasis on sex here is a problem that can be approached in a round-about way by considering the second peculiarity of Book 5. Aristotle announces early in the book that

> since we are considering from what civil wars (*staseis*) and revolutions (*metabolai*) concerning regimes come to be, let us first grasp their principles (*arkhai*) and causes (*aitiai*) in general. (1302a16–19)

The key terms in this passage are striking in their ambiguity. *Metabolê* can mean change or motion in addition to revolution. *Stasis*, as its English cognates suggest, can also mean rest. When regimes are in a state of civil unrest, they are paralyzed and so at rest. In a different context, then, Aristotle's statement of what he is doing in Book 5 might be understood to mean that he is inquiring into the causes and principles of motion and rest as they pertain to regimes. What is peculiar about all of this is that this is precisely the account Aristotle elsewhere gives of the science of nature.[77] Physics, the science of *phusis* (nature), is the study of the causes and principles of motion and rest. Does this mean that Book 5, which is about revolution, is about the nature of the *polis*? Put differently, with regard to the *polis*, rest (*stasis*) and motion (*metabolê*) are one. The nature of the *polis* is change.

Perhaps the most difficult problem for Aristotle in the *Physics* is the status of the accidental—chance. He is similarly preoccupied in *Politics* Book 5, where the examples are full of small things which for accidental reasons become big things and so cause revolution[78]: "Every difference is likely to make for dissension (*diastasin*)" (1303b14). Accordingly, even accidental differences are divisive. Aristotle takes up the issue of chance in his brief criticism at the end of Book 5 of the treatment of revolution in Plato's *Republic*. Beginning in Book 8 of the *Republic*, Socrates gives an account of the deterioration of the best regime, which he has just finished describing. The cause of this decline is supposed to be the failure to regulate births sufficiently to ensure that the best people will mate at precisely the right time so as to produce the best offspring. Socrates gives an elaborate mathematical account of what is called the "nuptial number," which is supposed to reveal the proper time to mate. However, the account is so elaborate and so nearly unintelligible as to be a sort of caricature of what would be necessary to maintain the regime. The perfect regime requires a science of generation so exact as to eliminate chance altogether and in particular chance as manifested in the erotic affairs of men. Aristotle agrees with Socrates in doubting the possibility of such a science but makes explicit that one must also doubt that changes of regime—the genesis or birth of one regime out of another—can be so perfectly predictable as they appear to be in the *Republic*. A science perfectly predicting change is as problematic as a science perfectly preventing it; for both, chance is the obstacle.

In Book 5 Aristotle always begins with the causes of each kind of revolution and then moves to the means for preserving the regimes in question. Preservation is presented as a reaction to the threat of change. Kingship, certainly the oldest of the regimes, is presented as having come to be for the purpose of assisting the better class against the people—the *dêmos* (1310b7–14). In fact, Aristotle goes out of his way to indicate that revolution is always negatively determined. He begins Book 5 with the claim that revolution comes to be as the result of a perceived injustice. But if the truth of the *polis*—of political society—is change, and Book 5 really points to the nature of the political, then all regimes come to be as the result of a perceived injustice. Not simply revolution, but political life as such will be negatively determined. Every regime takes its characteristic shape as a reaction to a perceived injustice; it is not determined by a notion of justice positively understood. Now, if the problem is that all politics, as a response to a perceived threat, is negatively determined, the question is, "What is the threat?" The answer has something to do with human sexuality in its connection with our awareness of our own partiality. This is why sex is so prominent in *Politics* Book 5.

Book 5 is the book on revolutions, which naturally enough points to the primordial revolution. Put somewhat differently, politics is the sign of desiring to be in control of our fates. It is in this sense that the goal of all political regimes, and so of all changes in regimes, is freedom. However, the gods are the sign that we are not in control. Their rule means our incompleteness. Although the gods have their purposes, theirs are not simply ours, or not perceivably so, for the gods do not show themselves as fundamentally different from chance. They rule us, and we cannot do anything about it. In the context of a comparison between kingship and tyranny, Aristotle indicates the problem: "Unwanted, a king will not be [a king], but tyrant is [a tyrant] even unwanted (1313a14–16). As permanent rulers whose rule does not depend on our consent, the gods are like tyrants. Consequently, the desire for freedom in its most extreme form will ultimately lead to a revolution against the gods.

Aristotle is, of course, familiar with the mythical account of such a revolution that Plato places in the mouth of the comic poet Aristophanes in the *Symposium*.[79] It is a revolution the consequence of which is the origin of *erôs*, which, according to Aristophanes, is identical to the origin of human beings as we know them.[80] As Aristophanes tells it, we were originally spherical in shape and came in three sexes—male, female, and androgyne. We had two faces, four arms, four legs, and two sexual organs. While it was possible for us to move by walking erect as we do now, it was more efficient to extend our members and circle like wheels. There was reproduction—females seem to have laid eggs on the ground where males deposited their sperm—but no sex. These circle-men attacked the Olympian gods for reasons very dark, except that they had "big thoughts" (the phrase appears earlier in the *Symposium* and is associated with the tyrannicides, Harmodius and Aristogeiton). As is always the case when one attacks the gods, the circle-men lost. Zeus decided to punish them by splitting them down the middle so that they would be both weaker and more numerous. That way he would have more worshippers and less troublesome ones. It is a very elegant solution. However, Zeus failed to foresee that these half-men would be so consumed with longing for their severed halves that, upon finding them, they would spend all their time hugging and longing to be made wholes and so would completely forget to eat. To keep the race from dying out, Zeus moved our sexual organs to the front and changed our manner of reproduction so that in this rebellious act of hugging, one thing would lead to another, and the result would be not the death of the species, but its reproduction. This was the origin of *erôs*.

Aristophanes' speech contains much more, but a few things can be said on the basis of this sketch. The myth seems at first to be an account of *erôs* as the longing of our impaired natures for their original wholeness, yet this does not explain why these circle-men were so dissatisfied as to revolt in the first place. If we were originally whole, why were we rebellious? And when we are halves, is any satisfaction really possible for us? A careful look at the details suggests that both original halves probably could not have survived. And certainly there can be no matching halves now. Zeus cuts the circle-men in half and then orders Apollo to sew them up, gathering the extra skin together like a purse. As Leo Strauss points out, one has to wonder where the extra skin comes from. Repairing one half seems to require the skin from the other. If so, for one half to live means the other must perish. Be that as it may, beginning in the second generation, there would in any event be no possibility in principle of finding one's true other half, for we would have been born as halves for which there is no natural completion. Accordingly, even were we to find what we believed to be our other half and "recombine," we would not be satisfied. For Aristophanes, then, *erôs* is the illusion that a particular beloved would make us whole and happy, and *erôs* is the essence of human beings as we now know them. *Erôs* saves us from despair; the hope it gives us makes us happy, paradoxically, happier than the circle-men who originally rebelled against the gods. They rebelled not out of any positive desire, but out of a negative sense of their own incompleteness. The circle-men could not bear not to be gods. For Aristophanes, *erôs* is a useful illusion rooted in something deeper, something closer to a general sense of discontent, an awareness of oneself as lacking that takes the form of anger at what is other than oneself.

Aristophanes, however, takes us still deeper. *Erôs* is a longing to couple with another human being in order to overcome one's own partiality—in order to become whole. According to his account, this wholeness is so desirable that we are willing to merge completely with our beloved. But this sacrifice of the self in a larger whole is not different in kind from what the political community demands of its citizens. It is this context in which Aristotle cites Aristophanes' speech in the *Politics* (1262b). And in the *Symposium* Aristophanes makes a point of connecting the activities of male halves to politics (192a). *Erôs* is indeed a longing for wholeness, but the "objective correlative" of this wholeness is not a circle-man but the *polis*. The *polis* is an ugly many-membered unit (compare 1290b25–40) in which the self is necessarily suppressed and ultimately, in the perfect *polis*, would be lost. There is no difference in principle between combining with one to overcome one's incompleteness and combining with many. The political community is therefore a vehicle for human autonomy. However, insofar as the *polis* is a coming together for the sake of autonomy, it is a new rebellion against what the gods represent. Rebelling against our lack of autonomy is a rebellion against the role that chance plays in our lives.

This "solution" to our incompleteness brings problems of its own. The wholeness of the political order depends totally on what it is a response to. The ugly core of patriotism is hatred of what is other. In addition, to form this artificial whole requires obedience to law. Men must submit to the rule of law for the sake of autonomy or freedom. This is the true meaning of Zeus's knife, that we can be free only by submitting to Zeus—conventional law. While this has rather obvious difficulties as a way to autonomy, it does begin to explain why the *polis* is always only a partial overcoming of our impaired condition. The law is a constant reminder that we must give up some of our freedom in order to be free. Political life is both the vehicle for and the obstacle to human freedom.

Now, what has all of this to do with Aristotle's *Politics* and with the larger issue of revolution? Aristophanes' speech suggests that man as man originated with the imposition of law. Civilization means submission to law for an essentially rebellious motive, the recovery of wholeness. It is therefore rooted in a perceived sense of injustice or violation. This essentially reactive character of politics is manifest in all regimes, but is perhaps most completely revealed in tyranny. Political life, built on a desire not to be ruled, requires submission to rule. Therefore, within the *polis* some will rule and some will be ruled, and so, within the *polis*, not to be ruled will mean to rule. Political life transforms our original desire not to be ruled into a desire to rule. One becomes conscious of one's own freedom in the act of ruling others.[81] Politically, this transformation of the desire for freedom into the desire to rule manifests itself externally as the desire for empire and internally as the desire to be a tyrant. Wherever Zeus is present as a sanction for the law, he is also present as a model for imitation. Without a sanction, the law is powerless; with a sanction, it is dangerous. All law, therefore, contains an antinomian element. Every time parents tell their children not to do something, they run the risk of simultaneously suggesting the possibility of doing it. And while children may obey when threatened with punishment, they may also long to be in the

position of the punisher. The problem, then, is that the freedom that
is the goal of political life is essentially negative in character. It is
rooted in a reactive passion, a desire not to be ruled. For that reason it generates an anger, a righteous indignation, which has as its
object the overcoming of whatever opposes it. But that is only to
say that this anger has ruling as its object. However, wherever there
are rulers, there will be some who are ruled. And wherever some
are ruled, regardless of the justice of the rule, there will be a perception of injustice. This, in turn, will generate a righteous indignation and, potentially, a new revolution with new rulers and so on.
All of this is what Aristotle has in mind by suggesting that the nature of the *polis* is revolution and by connecting revolution with
frustrated *erôs*. The very passion that is at the heart of political life
ensures imperfect satisfaction with political life.

Aristotle does not really wait until Book 5 to introduce this difficulty. It is present in various forms throughout the *Politics*, but
perhaps most startlingly in the ambiguous treatment of kingship at
the end of Book 3. As we have seen, the complete solution of the
political problem first seems to be the rule of the very best human
beings solely for the benefit of those whom they rule. And, since
good human beings are few, and there is only one best, the perfect
regime will be a species of monarchy. Ignoring for the moment the
enormous number of practical difficulties with a regime of this sort,
it does seem to embody the theoretical goal of the best political
order—the coincidence of wisdom and power. We have seen that
Aristotle indicates his awareness of the difficulty with this "best"
solution by likening this sort of king, the *pambasileus*, to the father
of a family (1285b33). Yet Book 1 is devoted in large part to the
argument that the kind of rule existing within the family is incomplete and not really political at all. Paternal rule, were it final, would
place children in a position of perpetual minority; they would be
like natural slaves. And as Book 1 makes quite clear, slavery is only
just when the slave is by nature suited to be ruled, a condition re-
alized only when the slave is not fully human. Aristotle's natural
slaves are mental incompetents. In Book 3 Aristotle indicates that
this is precisely the problem with kingship. If one understands the
goal of politics to be the efficient functioning of the political order,
the perfect unity of the regime, then no doubt the king can make
the trains run on time, but the cost is the dehumanizing of everyone else within the *polis*. The genuine superiority of the king prevents the citizens he governs from being as complete human beings

as they otherwise might be. In relation to the king, they are as natural slaves to their masters.

One might summarize the teaching of the *Politics* as a whole in
the following way. The first three books, which culminate in Aristotle's teaching about kingship, have as their underlying theme the
fact that the best regime is not really a regime. Its citizens are not
really human. Books 4–6 have as their underlying theme that the
best regime is not best. Inefficiency is the price that must be paid
for freedom, and hence humanity. Books 1–3 show that it is unjust
for the best men not to rule. Books 4–6 show that it is unjust for
them to rule. Not only will the *polis* always be perceived as unjust;
it will always be unjust. The final two books of the *Politics* deal
with the consequences for the *polis* of an awareness of the necessarily imperfect character of the *polis*.

This whole issue can be seen slightly differently. Book 5 of the
Politics is especially concerned with tyranny. Tyrants are usually
hated and killed in the name of some alternative political order,
frequently a restoration. Brutus and Cassius, so different in all else,
are united in their wish to restore the republic so that they will not
have to be ruled by another human being. Aristotle is preoccupied
with tyranny in Book 5 because it is simply the most extreme form
of what makes regimes change. Granted that tyranny is illegitimate
rule, in some sense all rule will be perceived as illegitimate, and
hence tyrannical. Tyranny points to the fact that revolution must be
understood as rooted in a sense of violation of one's dignity, integrity, or wholeness. This need for integrity is the fundamental source
of political life and, at the same time, the source of the destruction
of political life. Tyranny is a sort of castration, like Zeus's castration of men. The demand for justice is rooted in our sense of our
own castration.[82]

In Book 4 this difficulty is presented as a tension between the
political order as a whole and its parts understood as citizens. We
belong to the *polis* out of a desire to control our own lives; the
political association is formed for the purpose of overcoming the
rule of chance. The parts of the *polis* are meant to fit together like
the parts of a well-oiled machine. For the machine to be perfect
the parts must be perfect. But insofar as the tasks to be done are
heterogeneous, the perfect instruments to accomplish these tasks will
differ radically from one another. The perfectly functioning machine
is not an association of beings of the same kind; it is a whole composed of parts sharing nothing other than their common suppres-

sion in a whole. The underlying tragedy of the perfect *polis* is that the restoration of our wholeness would require that we become perfect parts, and so deny our wholeness altogether.

Our initial question had to do with the connection between tyranny and sexuality, and revolution. We have seen that for Aristotle tyranny points to the essentially revolutionary nature of the *polis*. But what is the connection of all of this to physics? The problem for Aristotelian physics—chance or the accidental—is also the obstacle to autonomy or freedom. If our goal is autonomy, then the only complete solution would be mastery of the whole of which we are parts. Aristotle's concluding criticism of Plato's "nuptial number" is meant to indicate the impossibility of overcoming chance. The criticism is thus connected to tyranny since the tyrant is simply the manifestation of the ultimate failure of politics as a means to regain control of our lives. Killing a tyrant in anger is the human attempt to regain control, an attempt perfectly justifiable but still bound to fail. Like the mythical attempt to kill the gods, it is a reenactment of our origins.

Recognizing the continuing importance of chance in human affairs undermines the tendency to think of any change as final. It is not an accident that our age, which takes so seriously the possibility of permanent change resulting from revolution, also takes for granted the existence of a physics designed to banish chance. For Aristotle chance is a permanent feature of human life. There is nevertheless a quintessentially human tendency to attempt to overcome chance. This tendency is rooted in the sense of righteous indignation that makes revolution possible. People do not like to go hungry or be abused, but revolution requires that they be angry about their hunger or abuse. Only when hunger becomes an insult are we willing to risk our lives to remove it. Otherwise, the logic of hunger tells us that it is better to be hungry than dead. We would refer to this as the role of ideology in revolution. Aristotle prefers to refer to it negatively as the perception of injustice. Righteousness, once aroused, is inclined to think in terms of the total removal of the evil that has aroused it; it thinks in terms of final solutions. Accordingly, righteousness aims at a change (*metabolê*) that will come to a rest (*stasis*). Its goal is necessarily extreme, but it would be as difficult to organize a revolution with moderation as its principle as it is to acknowledge moderation as the principle of polity.[83]

Aristotle's account of revolution (*metabolê*) is part of a larger account of change (*metabolê*) that has as its goal to make chance intelligible without doing away with its chance character. Book 4 began with a reflection on the relation between part and whole, the consequence of which was that the very notion of a science of the whole becomes problematic. This problem showed up in the *polis* as the difficulty of locating that "part"—the soul—that is the principle of the wholeness of the whole. Book 4 begins the part of the *Politics* concerned with "political science," but *politikê epistêmê* turns out to mean knowledge of why the *polis* is a necessarily imperfect being. This analysis continues in Book 5. The *polis* is essentially negative; it is rooted in a reactive passion—the desire not to be ruled. For this reason it generates an anger that has as its object overcoming whatever opposes it, i.e., ruling. But ruling means that there will be those who are ruled, and being ruled always involves a perception of injustice that will itself generate a sense of righteous indignation serving as a cause of *metabolê*. Movement or change is thus the essence of the *polis*. Revolution is born from a sense of the violation of integrity; righteous indignation is a demand for wholeness. But we have no other way of becoming perfectly whole than by becoming perfect parts. The problem of Book 5 is therefore simply another version of the part/whole problem of Book 4. Aristotle goes out of his way to make clear that it is also the problem of physics. Because of the necessary presence of chance, in the end, physics itself begins to look like knowledge of ignorance. Once again, politics and philosophy strangely mirror one another.

Chapter Six

Democracy and the Haphazard: *Politics* Book 6

The first three books of the *Politics* consider the *polis* from the point of view of its perfection. Accordingly, Book 3 culminates in an account of kingship as a form of familial—that is, non-political—rule. The *polis*, like the beings for whom it is the comprehensive association, is a class jumper. It is the sort of being that can only be understood in terms of a perfection to which it points but which is quite other than it and excludes it. The best city is not a city. The subject of *Politics* 1-3 is, therefore, political philosophy—an account of the being of the city, of the city at rest, even though the city can never be at rest.[84] *Politics* 4-6 considers the *polis* as a *polis*—as a being the very being of which is to be in motion and so necessarily imperfect. Beginning in Book 4, Aristotle refers to this account of the political in its own terms as political science or knowledge. It is an attempt to describe a structure of change (itself at rest) that will be an account of the necessary motion of any city. The best city is not best. This second part of the *Politics* culminates in a more elaborate consideration of democracy, although it is not at first blush clear why. That is, having treated democracy in various ways in Books 3, 4, and 5, why does Aristotle think it necessary to return to it at such length in Book 6?

This problem is especially acute given the way Aristotle begins Book 6. After summarizing Books 4-5, he remarks that there hap-

pen or chance to be various species of democracy and similarly of
other regimes and that he might as well (literally that it would not
be worse to) take a look at what's left (1316b36–40). Book 6 therefore introduces itself as an afterthought—a book of leftovers. Giv-
en how carefully Aristotle has constructed the rest of the *Politics*,
we are moved to wonder whether there might be a connection between democracy and the haphazard.

At least the connection to the preceding book is fairly clear. Book
5 showed that the cause of revolution or change (*metabolê*) in political life was the same as the cause of the origin of political life—
a perception of injustice. Men perceive any rule at all as an affront
to their dignity or wholeness. Ironically, political life originates when
men organize themselves as a group, and so submit to rule, in order to counteract the sense of injustice rooted in every experience
of being ruled.[85] Political life is born of a longing to be free.[86] But
the regime that openly claims freedom as its principle (*hupothesis*)
is democracy, and men are accustomed to say that only in this regime is there participation in freedom (1317a40–b1). Accordingly,
given the discoveries of Book 5, Aristotle must reconsider democracy in light of its claim to be the single legitimate regime, the only
regime openly devoted to the true goal of political life—freedom.
This seems to be why Aristotle can say that

> since there happen to be several species of democracy and of
> other regimes similarly, we may as well [or: "it is not worse to"]
> both investigate whether anything remains concerning them and at
> the same time assign [*apodidômi*: give back] the proper and useful
> way regarding each. (1316b36–40)

The two issues central to Book 5—chance and freedom—reemerge
and are brought into agreement as the form and the matter of
Book 6.

According to Book 5, the principle of politics is something like
"you can't do that to me"—an expression used only when you have
already succeeded in doing "that" to me. But freedom negatively
determined induces a secret longing for tyranny. Our freedom from
others makes itself felt in our rule over them. Because politics so
understood seems tragic, Aristotle turns in Book 6 to a reconsideration of freedom as the principle of political life. Book 5 leads us
to wonder to what extent freedom can be determined positively, and
Book 4 leads us to wonder to what extent it can be openly and fully

articulated as the principle of a regime. The book on democracy is therefore their natural completion.

A positive understanding of the regime devoted to freedom would require at least that democracy neither be nor understand itself as rule of the poor. The *dêmos* cannot rule justly as a class—as a part— any more than any other class can rule according to its understanding of what is good for itself or for the whole. Rather, that all perceive themselves as free must mean that none think themselves sufficiently powerful to impose their wills on others. Accordingly, in democracy "doing what you want" must give way to "not being forced to do what you do not want." But is this a coherent principle by which to order a regime or a life? After all, only if you want to do something else will you know that you are being forced to do what you do not wish to do. But for freedom to be positively determined, and felt as such, it must consist in something more than not being forced. I want to do what I want to do; anything less will not satisfy me. By making freedom its principle, democracy gives the appearance of neutrality to the ends it makes possible—the Declaration of Independence celebrates the pursuit of happiness, not happiness itself.

Only by making freedom appear to be an end in its own right, independent of what it is freedom for, can democracy present itself as the best regime. Book 6 explores the possibility of such a presentation, but the problem it faces is severe. Freedom to do what one wishes, and do so self-consciously, requires that one articulate the idiosyncratic principles according to which one lives, but this means ordering one's life according to certain principles—acknowledged or not. To live by a principle (*arkhê*) is to introduce rule or sovereignty (*arkhê*), and so to introduce being ruled. The very exercise of freedom makes feeling free problematic. From the point of view of the lawgiver, giving a law to oneself is liberating; from the point of view of him receiving the law it is an act of submission that, according to Book 5, induces resentment. Book 6 considers freedom from the point of view of the lawgiver; it is probably not accidental that Aristotle will be silent about the status of the lawgiver in Books 7–8. Feeling free and being free, thinking and doing, are once again at odds.

The structure of Book 6 mirrors this issue. The explicit reconsideration of democracy occupies most of the book and divides into accounts of the causes of democracy (chapter 1), freedom as the principle or hypothesis of democracy (chapter 2), equality (chapter 3), the kinds of democracy (chapter 4), and the preservation of democracy (chapter 5). In chapters 6–7 Aristotle considers oligarchy and democracy together, and in chapter 8 he turns to the question of offices, not just in democracy but apparently in any city whatsoever. The most obvious difficulty is chapter 8. Why does a book that deals almost exclusively with democracy end with an account of political offices in general? Furthermore, it is not at once clear why Aristotle introduces a new discussion of the relation of oligarchy to democracy, as though a consideration of the two independently were impossible. In general, Book 6 could be said to move from a discussion of freedom to a discussion of rule (*arkhê*). That the discussion of democracy leads willy-nilly to a discussion of oligarchy and the discussion of freedom leads similarly to a discussion of rule will prove a sign of the instability of freedom as a political principle.

Aristotle sets a double goal for Book 6. Not only will he examine what is useful relative to the various species of democracies (1316b36–40), he will also consider the various possible combinations of the species mentioned (1316b40–1317a1). Yet, as many have pointed out, Aristotle does not seem to address this second issue.[87] Accordingly, it is customary to treat Book 6 as unfinished.[88] But is this second issue really missing? If all democracies were already necessarily "combinations" of other regimes, then perhaps Book 6 would be complete. This thought is not as strange as it at first seems. At 1317a4–10 Aristotle explains what he has in mind.

> I mean (*legô*) those couplings which ought to be investigated but are not now investigated, for example, were the part deliberating and that concerning the selection of offices organized oligarchically but the things concerning the courts aristocratically; or these and that concerning deliberation oligarchically, but that concerning selections aristocratically; or if in some other way not all the things proper [*oikeia*: akin] to the *politeia* were put together.

Curiously, Aristotle cites no democratic example, whether deliberative, judicial, or connected with the selection of offices. Is all order necessarily nondemocratic? We must look to the sequel.

> What sort of democracy suits what sort of *polis*, and similarly also of oligarchies what sort [is suited] to what multitude, and of the rest of the regimes which is advantageous to which has been said before. (1317a11–13)

Aristotle couples a sort of democracy with a sort of *polis*—that is, with a *polis* already understood as having a form, and so, presumably, a *politeia*. He couples oligarchy not with a *polis* but with a *plêthos*—a multitude. There does not seem to be any pure democracy; rule is in principle hierarchical. If someone walks into a room of five hundred people, announces that they have been given full authority to design and institute a national health plan, and then promptly leaves the room, how will these five hundred people proceed to exercise the power they have been granted? Authority was given them as a *plêthos*, but as an aggregate of individuals, each having an equal say, they are powerless. To act they must organize themselves—selecting a chair, stipulating rules of procedure, and so on. But any of this will, at least for a time, place one or more of them in positions of authority over others. Someone will have to propose these organizational measures and so take the lead, and someone will have to decide when procedures have been followed. And of course, before they can select a health plan, they must first make concrete proposals. Some will draft these proposals; others will simply react to them. In each of these instances, an inequality of roles will have been established.

Never altogether pure, any actual democracy is always already in some way "oligarchic." Where there is rule, some rule others and are in some way "few" relative to the many who are ruled.

> But since it nevertheless must become clear of these regimes not only what sort is best for *poleis*, but also how both these and others must be instituted, let us attack it briefly (*suntomôs*). And first let us speak about democracy. For at the same time what concerns the regime laid down in opposition [*antikeimenês*: corresponding] to it is evident, and this is what some call oligarchy. (1317a14–18)

The regime laid down in opposition to democracy is at the same time the regime that corresponds to democracy. Democracy and "so-called oligarchy" are intimately linked. It is not just that a non-egalitarian political possibility stands in opposition to egalitarian democracy. Some call the regime opposed to democracy oligarchy, but, because any *politeia* will be both in opposition to and correspond to the principle of democracy—freedom—in some sense the principle of all regimes is at odds with all regimes.

At the end of the first chapter, Aristotle turns to the two kinds of causes for the variety of democracies. On the one hand this duality of cause is clear.

> For there are two causes on account of which democracies are
> various, first the one said before, that the *dêmoi* are different. . . .
> (1317a23–25)

As the character (*êthos*) of the *dêmos* varies, it will want different
things. A farming *dêmos* will not want what a manufacturing *dêmos* wants. If freedom is understood to be doing what one wants,
then the nature of particular democracies will vary radically depending on the *êthos* of the *dêmos*. A *polis* with a citizen body more or
less homogeneous economically, racially, and religiously will scarcely have to cultivate tolerance as a virtue. Freedom as doing what
you want is a lot easier when you all want the same things.

> The second is the one concerning which we now speak. For the
> things following democracies and seeming to be proper (*oikeia*) for
> this regime, when combined, make democracies different. For in
> one fewer will follow, in another more, and in another all these.
> (1317a29–33)

Certain institutions are typical of democratic rule—for example,
election by lot and absence of property qualifications for voting.
Some of these institutions will be present in some democratic regimes and some in others. As their combinations vary, so too will
the democracies in which they are combined vary in terms of who
rules whom. The double cause of variety in democracy thus corresponds to a doubleness within the democratic understanding of
freedom. On the one hand freedom means being ruled and ruling
in turn (1317b2–3); on the other, it means to live as one
wishes (1317b12). When what one wishes varies, the character of
the democracy will vary, as it also will when the institutions of
rule vary.

But there is a second, less obvious aspect to this dualism:
"What must remain for this inquiry are all the things of the *dêmos* (*ta dêmotika*) and the things seeming to follow democracies"
(1317a19–21). This distinction is in some way related to the concluding sentence of chapter one: "Let us now speak of the things
thought worthy [claims: *ta axiômata*], characters (*ta êthê*) and what
they aim at" (1317a39). The characters that democracies have are
not simply the same as their claims—what they hold up as worthy.
Since what they aim at differs from what they understand themselves to aim at, an ambiguity is present in "doing what one wish-

es." Democratic institutions self-consciously aim at achieving certain results, at causing certain effects; at the same time, these institutions are the effects of a democratic *êthos*.

Aristotle lists eleven "things following democracy": all choosing those to hold offices from all; all ruling each and each all by turns; selection to offices by lot (or at least those not involving special expertise); no property qualification for citizenship (or a small one); a prohibition against holding offices more than once (or allowing for this only rarely, such as for military offices); short terms for all offices (where possible); all judging by those selected from all and concerning everything (or at least the most important things); the sovereignty of the assembly in all (or the most important) matters; payment for holding all (or the most important) offices; emphasis on ill birth, poverty and vulgarity; no life offices (or those that exist stripped of power and chosen by lot) (1317b16–1318a2).

It is of some interest that the eleventh item of the list, no lifetime terms of office, is simply a special case of the sixth and central item, limited duration of terms of office. Both are designed to prevent some men from getting used to ruling and others to being ruled. At the same time, they draw our attention to what is perhaps the most powerful fiction of democracy (an effect of its *êthos*)—that offices (*arkhai*) rule (*arkhein*) and not men. "Being ruled and ruling in turn," therefore, has as its aim never really being ruled by another man and never ruling another man. While the list as a whole is a description of institutions with specific aims, all reflect the desire to make rule possible while minimizing the extent to which people are rulers.

That this is not altogether possible is clear from the way Aristotle regularly modifies his democratic principle when it conflicts with the demands of good rule. Offices, for example, are filled by lot except when they require great skill—that is, wisdom. Because the city is never simply indifferent to which person holds which office, it is never simply democratic. In the fully democratic city there could be no preference for the judgment of one citizen over that of another. Ultimately, this would mean the destruction of any power other than the will of *dêmos* assembled. However, even here the indifference to differences among citizens means only that, as each counts equally, fifty-one percent can tyrannize forty-nine percent. Counting everyone equal means that, in the end, everyone does not count equally.

The "things following democracies" are presented by Aristotle as effects of freedom, not its causes.

> These are the things common to democracies, for what especially seems to be democracy and the *dêmos* occurs as a result of the justice agreed to be democratic—and this is having everything equal according to number. (1318a3–7)

The institutions follow from democratic justice rather than causing it. Accordingly, when those who establish regimes seek to bring together everything that follows from the democratic principle, they err by treating effects as causes. While a sign that democracy is present may be that no man is considered so superior that he is elected to permanent office, this is not to say that laying down a law prohibiting anyone from holding permanent office will create a democratic regime. In the one case, the institution is a natural outgrowth of democracy; in the other, it may well be an acknowledgment of the existence of superiority and so be antidemocratic in a perverse way.

The character of democracy is not produced by its claims; rather, the claims, what is thought worthy, are produced by its character—what it wants but does not necessarily know that it wants. But democracy tends not to understand itself this way. Ordinarily, it confuses causes and effects in its legislation. Equality can be understood as an effect of justice insofar as it is rooted in freedom—no one lords it over others. Truly democratic legislation would establish conditions that engender in citizens a sense of equality based on a sense of freedom. But this is not the same as legislation establishing institutions that assume equality. Equalizing property by legal confiscation is no guarantee of democratic justice; it is an attempt to legislate an effect as though it were a cause. However, because democracy more than any other regime seems to be based on an idea, this difference between legislating causes and legislating effects is difficult to maintain. A regime based on an idea runs the risk of substituting the proclamation of this idea for legislation designed to implement it. In its wholesale substitution of democratic institutions for the democratic *êthos*, it substitutes philosophy for politics.

Democracy tends to place great faith in legislated institutions because its moral foundation is an idea—a universal claim about freedom.

The hypothesis of the democratic regime, then, is freedom. And they are accustomed to say this—that in this regime alone is there participation in freedom, for they assert that every democracy aims at this. (1317a40–b2)

Aristotle is apparently not altogether convinced either that democracy leads to participation in freedom or that every democracy aims at it. Part of the difficulty is that, as we have already seen, democratic freedom means two things.

And one [aspect] of freedom is being ruled and ruling in turn; and demotic justice is standing equal according to number but not according to worth (*axian*), and, when this is the just, the multitude necessarily is sovereign, and whatever the multitude may resolve [whatever may seem to the multitude] this is the end and this is the just, for they say it is necessary that each of the citizens have equal standing. (1317b2–8)

And one is living as one wishes; for they assert this to be the function (*ergon*) of freedom, if indeed not living as one wishes belongs to a slave. Of democracy then this is the second marker. (1317b11–14)

The first understanding of freedom derives from the second since

from this [the second] has come not being ruled, especially not by anyone, unless in turn, and it contributes in this way toward the freedom according to equality. (1317b14–17)

In one way, this is fairly clear. Freedom understood as ruling in turn, as equality, derives from freedom as doing what one wishes. Freedom as equality is meant to be a means to freedom as doing what one wishes, not its expression. Yet the means is ultimately at odds with that for which it is the means. Pure democracy is a majoritarian tyranny. Accordingly, the regime with the most democratic institutions will not necessarily be the most democratic. No one wishes to be forced to be free.

This derivative status of democratic political institutions can also be understood differently. Democracy is the regime that least distinguishes between rulers and ruled. When Aristotle repeatedly and rather pointedly ignores the difference between *democratia* and the *dêmos*[89], he is only treating democracy democratically, for the form and matter of the *polis* are not easily distinguished where the people can say "we are the city." But where there is no clear sense of the difference between rulers and ruled, there will be no clear sense of the recalcitrance of the matter of the *polis*, individual human beings, to its form, the *politeia*—of the ruled to rule. For this reason democracies are especially prone to believe that what seems (*dokei*) to them is so resolved (*dokei*) and so comes to be—as though an act of Congress by its mere enactment describes something actual. For democracy, the distance between *logos* and *ergon*, between speech and deed, seems perilously small. As this is never really the case, however, democracy is particularly vulnerable to chance. Rather than closing the gap between doing and thinking, the regime most based on an idea, because it fails to acknowledge the power of the accidental, falls most prey to it.

Democracy's hypothesis is freedom. But freedom means either doing what one wishes or ruling and being ruled in turn. Now, ruling and being ruled in turn is simply the equivalent, on the level of the regime, to doing what one wishes. In democracy, in principle, there is no ruler, and thus no one is ruled. Because whatever the regime wills—what seems to it—is, ruling and being ruled in turn represents the complete victory of will over intelligence. But because, given such a triumph of the will, there is no *polis*, political life requires that the democratic hypothesis be tempered. Aristotle turns to this issue in chapter 3.

Stable political life requires minimizing the feeling that we are ruled by others, lest we inevitably have the "big thoughts" of Aristophanes' circle-men, resent being ruled, and rebel. At the same time political life does mean being ruled. Book 6 begins by acknowledging our demand for freedom but then gradually moderates it so as to make rule possible.[90] This amounts to recasting the question of equality to avoid the tyranny of the majority.

> For it is equal for the poor (*aporoi*) to rule no more than the well-off (*euporoi*) nor to have sovereignty alone but for all [to rule] from the equal according to number. For thus they would hold both equality and freedom to exist with respect to the *politeia*. And after this it is asked [*aporeitai*: it is needed], "How do they stand with respect to the equal?" (1318a7–12)

Aristotle calls attention to the etymological connection between the poor (*aporoi*) and the verb to question (*aporeisthai*) here and does so again at the conclusion of chapter three: "For the weaker always seek the equal and the just, while the strong give it no thought [*ouden phrontizousin*: think nothing]" (1318b5–6). Those who ask must feel a lack; they must be in need. The articulation of justice as the goal of political life is, therefore, more likely to come to sight in democracy than in any other regime. Democracy is steeped in the question of justice.

Democracy demands equality, but rule of any sort means inequality. The question, then, is what sort of inequality best serves the demand for equality. Clearly, if democracy stands for anything it stands for the rule of the *dêmos*—the people—and the majority has the most obvious claim to be the voice of the people. But the simple rule of the majority leads to tyranny, violating the hypothesis of democracy—freedom. Aristotle therefore introduces a more complicated understanding of the rule of the majority.

> After this is asked, How do they stand with respect to the equal? Ought the estimations [*timêmata*: property estimates or honorings] of five hundred be distinguished from a thousand and the thousand have equal power with the five hundred? Or ought it not be disposed thus with respect to this equality but be distinguished thus: after taking equal numbers from the five hundred and the thousand, these would be sovereign over elections and courts? (1318a11–17)

Timêma, connected to the verb to honor, is one of those words like *arkhê* that in Athens have both a general and a technical meaning.[91] It means something like honor or esteem, but is used more particularly to refer to the assessment made of a citizen's property for purposes of taxation. Most obviously at issue here is whether all citizens should be strictly equal—one man, one vote—or whether voting should reflect the relative wealth of citizens as indicated by their property assessments. Yet the less technical meaning of *timêma* is also present, for beneath the question of property assessments lies the question of what makes a citizen worthy of honor. Aristotle means to temper the strictly egalitarian principle of democracy, but he sees two ways to accomplish this end. One might establish an assembly in which the poor (the thousand) and the rich (the five hundred) both participate, but in which the five hundred and the thousand hold equal power. It would then become clear to the meanest intelligence that each of the rich counts for two of the poor. The alternative is to choose a group made up equally of rich and poor to govern. The result would be the same insofar as the rich would be represented in a proportion double to that of the poor, but, as each member would have one vote, an appearance of equality would be preserved. Within the group, each would have an equal voice. In both these cases Aristotle presents the basis for what has been called "a concurrent majority of poor and rich."[92] While it might seem that democratic justice requires rule of the multitude (*plêthos*) and that oligarchic justice is based on the magnitude of property or being (*plêthos ousias*), both of these are unstable. Because it does not esteem or honor the individual citizen as individual, oligarchic justice in principle sanctions the rule not of the few but of the single most wealthy man. If it is not freedom but *ousia* that justifies rule, it would seem that either the multitude would have more of it than the few rich, or the single richest would, by virtue of being richest, have the right to rule. In the end, oligarchy collapses either into democracy or into tyranny because it contains no coherent account of what makes an individual citizen an individual.[93] Democracy, on the other hand, leads to the unjust and repeated confiscation of the *ousia* of the rich by the poor. It is so concerned with freedom as not being ruled that it cannot afford to acknowledge that some citizens bring more to the *polis* than others. Anything concretely setting one citizen apart from another threatens the fundamental equality of democracy. There can be no "distinguished citizens" because the sovereignty of the *dêmos* is based on the lowest common denominator of its individual members, on their freedom as such and not on any further qualification of this lowest common denominator—any property or being that belongs to them.

If rule of the *plêthos* destroys freedom, the hypothesis of democracy, then whatever arrangement preserves democracy will be more democratic. In this way, Aristotle argues that his "concurrent majorities," according to which neither the poor nor the rich can act with utter disregard for the other, are more democratic. On a practical level, this makes some sense; one can see its legacy in various bicameral legislatures around the world. On a theoretical level it also makes sense; the egalitarian absolute freedom to do what one wants cannot show itself apart from doing something in particular, thereby distinguishing oneself.

Democracies vary depending on how the democratic principle is modified so as to make a democratic regime possible. Here (1318b7) Aristotle refers to four sorts of democracy, but in Book 4 (1291b29–1292a5) he listed five: one where all share rule—even the rich; one

with a small property qualification for citizenship; one where those
of good birth rule and law is sovereign; one where all rule but law
is sovereign; one where the *plêthos* rules without law. The discrep-
ancy disappears if we understand the first of the five, where all
share in rule or offices, to be the hypothesis of democracy generally and the remaining four to be ways of instituting this hypothesis.
The last, the rule of the multitude without law is on the one hand
most democratic, but since

> where laws do not rule, there is not a *politeia* . . . , if democracy is
> one of the *politeiai*, it is apparent that such a system, in which
> everything is managed by decree, is not even authoritatively [*kuriôs*:
> sovereignly] a democracy. . . . (1292a32–37)

The most "democratic" is not really a regime and so not really
democratic. A discussion of real democracies thus involves an account of the ways in which they have been oligarchized.

The best democracy is one in which the citizens are farmers.
The *êthos* of the country involves acknowledging necessity. While
in the city, because everything around us has been transformed from
its natural state, the conditions of our existence may seem infinite-
ly malleable, farmers are aware of how much they depend on nature's caprice. They also have little leisure because they have little
property (*ousia*). Farmers need to work to acquire the necessities
and would be impatient were they to have to spend much time in
the assembly. They prefer gain to honor, and, if they have any hint
of love of honor, it shows itself as the desire not to be pushed
around. Accordingly, a farming *dêmos* will be content with the power
to elect and audit. Their preference for gain over honor is a sign
that although they may be poor, these farmers take no pride in poverty and indeed wish to be rich. They do not demand honor for what
they are minimally—individuals stripped of all property. Aristotle's
description suggests that the real virtue of a farming democracy is
that it has all the advantages of oligarchic institutions without establishing them by law. Those more able to rule do so but not because anyone is excluded from rule. The *dêmos* will have neither
the time nor the inclination to do more than act as a check on the
rich. They will not seek to substitute their will for the law and at
the same time will be sufficiently powerful to prevent the rich from
acting simply as they wish. Ironically, this compromise—that nei-

ther the rich nor the poor will be able to do whatever they wish—
makes for the best democracy, the regime that has as its principle
freedom or doing as one wishes. The regime will be doubly good
because this arrangement occurs naturally and is not the result of
design. Neither the *dêmos* nor the rich will be dishonored; the one
does not wish to rule, and the other is not insulted by being excluded from rule.

To encourage a healthy democracy, then, means to encourage
farming. Laws that proclaim equality will only engender resentment;
laws designed to make it difficult to acquire great amounts of
land so that landowners will be working farmers or those designed
to prevent any citizen from selling his allotment of land will be indirectly democratic. To encourage farming as a way of life is
to affect how people will vote—what they will want—without
depriving them of their freedom to vote as they wish. They will
understand themselves as, and be, free, but their way of life will
be the cause of their freedom rather than their freedom being the
cause of their way of life. If democracy is the regime that celebrates freedom, the best democracy is the one that misunderstands
what makes it free.

For various reasons a *dêmos* of farmers is not always possible.
Democratic justice will scarcely be served by forcing a nonagricul-
tural people into the fields; it would be hard to justify this in terms
of the principle of doing what one wishes. What then is to be done?
Since "almost all the other multitudes from which the remaining
democracies are constituted are much baser than these" (1319a24–
26), and "the power of doing what one wishes is not able to ward
off the base in each man" (1318b40–1319a20), a nonagrarian democracy will have within it the principle of its own instability. If
the *dêmos* consists of handicraftsmen (*hoi banausoi*—the vulgar),
merchants, and laborers, the very character of their activity will be
detrimental to the quality of their citizenship; it will encourage in
them the slavishness born of attempting to please those they serve.
At the same time, unlike farming, this activity will not serve as
a constant reminder of the limits of what is possible. Although
ill-suited for it, by hanging around the marketplace, such a *dêmos*
has ample opportunity for self-government. Preserving the regime
under these conditions proves to require a series of legal institutions. In the best democracy these institutions are least required.
Their place is taken by a sort of prepolitical oligarchic disposition.
Democracy, then, is as good as its citizen body, but, where this

goodness must be produced by institutions, the institutions are in-compatible with the fundamental principle of democracy understood as living as one wishes.

Democracy is preserved by oligarchic, not democratic, institu-tions. So Aristotle recommends, for example, that when property is confiscated it should not be placed in the public treasury, but in a separate sacred treasury. In this way fear of losing one's property will deter injustice among the rich, but the hope of gain will not encourage unjust confiscation among the poor.[94] If there are large penalties for frivolous lawsuits, then the number of suits will be few. This seems at first neutral to the distinction between rich and poor, but when one realizes that most suits are aimed at the rich, it becomes clear that this penalty is an oligarchic institution. And, while it may be necessary to pay the poor to attend the assembly, Aristotle recommends that the sessions be short so that the pay is not an excessive burden on the rich, whose taxes will have provid-ed the revenues for the payment. Finally, Aristotle proposes that when wealth is redistributed, it not be given equally to all a little at a time but rather in turn and in quantities sufficiently large to make a difference in the lives of those to whom it is given. When one of the poor receives enough to purchase a piece of land, he is no longer simply one of the poor. All of these provisions are oli-garchic checks on democracy designed to preserve democracies from their baser impulses.

It comes as no surprise then that Aristotle next moves to a dis-cussion of oligarchy and democracy considered together.

> Also concerning oligarchy how one must [institute it] is pretty much apparent from these things. For one must infer from opposites—each oligarchy being analogous to the opposite democracy. . . . (1320b18–21)

Oligarchy and democracy are two sides of one coin. Democracy emphasizes freedom, which in turn leads to equality, but equality taken absolutely results in the tyranny of the majority. Oligarchy is the necessary democratic supplement to too much democracy. The strength of democracy is its *poluanthrôpia*—its quantity of human beings (1321a1–2). The strength of oligarchy is its *eutaxia*—its good order (1321a3–4). Democracy provides the matter of political life, oligarchy the form. When the matter is naturally good, very little form is needed. Good men might live together under what seems a purely democratic regime. When men are bad, however, form is needed in proportion to their badness.

Aristotle concludes chapter five with the following sentence: "How one must (*dei*) construct (*kataskeuazein*) democracy, then, has been said" (1320b16–17). And he concludes chapter seven with this: "Let this way be defined, how one should (*khrê*), then, set democracies and oligarchies in order (*kathistanai*)" (1321b2–3). Constructing democracies requires attending to freedom as their fundamental principle. If one wishes to order them correctly, however, one would do well to pay attention to the necessary connection between democracy and oligarchy. There can be no political equality without hierarchy and no political hierarchy without equality. Where either is wanting by nature it must be shored up by artifice. This relation between order and equality is a matter of necessity; all that is open to us is whether we will acknowledge it or not.

Aristotle concludes Book 6 with an enumeration of offices. Since the book has been primarily concerned with democracy, we might expect these to be democratic offices. However, a quick look makes it clear that many would have to be present in any city, for

> apart from the necessary offices it is impossible for a city to be, and [apart from] those with a good order (*eutaxia*) and arrangement (*kosmos*) it is impossible to be managed beautifully. (1321b6–9)

Any office (*arkhê*) is a sign of rule (*arkhê*). Who rules whom is the most difficult problem for democracy. Aristotle's book on democracy thus illustrates its problem. One may begin with freedom and equality as political principles, but the logic of politics forces one to end by considering who will rule whom. The overall movement of Book 6 from equality to rule and from democracy to oligarchy therefore has a certain necessity to it and reflects political life itself.

One example perhaps best reveals Aristotle's understanding of the problem of democracy. It is the fifth in his list of nine offices.

> Coming after this is the most necessary and pretty much the most difficult of offices—the one concerning the actions of those condemned and of those summoned for trial and concerning the guarding of people [*sômata*: bodies]. (1321b40–1322a2)

This office is the most necessary because without the threat of punishment, the law will have no force. It is most difficult because it brings no honor and in fact arouses hatred. These men who punish and ultimately may be responsible for executing their fellows must be paid at a very high rate, for otherwise, given the odium their task inspires, they would be tempted not to do their jobs. This points to what men hate most about the *polis*—that it forcibly limits freedom. The office of punisher is most difficult in democracy—the regime that celebrates freedom. Theoretically, the most democratic way of filling the office would be to spread the odium around equally. All would be executors of the law and ultimately executioners; all would be the enemies of all. This, however, undermines the democratic *polis*. Since everyone would be my potential executioner, I would feel not free, but subject to everyone. In a democracy the most necessary and difficult task cannot be accorded the greatest honor. It is no accident that the Greek word for public executioner is *ho dêmios*; as an adjective it means "belonging to the *dêmos*." It is the paradigm for the problem of rule in democracy. The regime most devoted to an idea, and so philosophical, can least afford to be self-aware, and so philosophical. If philosophy is to make its way into the *polis* it will have to do so less directly.

Part III

Politics and Philosophy

Chapter Seven

Politics and Poetry: *Politics* Book 7

It is odd that the regime with the least political principle—doing whatever one wishes—should in its extreme form politicize everything. When the *dêmos* say, "We are the *polis*," the private sphere disappears, and everything gets understood in terms of justice or, in our age, rights. In a way, this is simply the consequence of the new beginning at the outset of Book 4. When we take our bearings by the necessarily defective character of all regimes, politics becomes aporetic—problematic; we understand ourselves as needy or poor—*aporoi*: "For the weaker always seek the equal and the just, but the strong give them no thought" (1318b5–6). On the other hand, the regime that at first seems most political ends by depoliticizing everything. The *pambasileus* of Book 3 is not so much a king as a father. He understands human beings in terms of what is good for them; the just disappears.

The whole structure of the *Politics* can be understood in terms of this tension between the just and the good. Regimes may take their bearings by freedom or by wisdom. Their emphasis is either on choosing the good or on doing the good. We have seen this before as the battle between knowing and doing.[95] In Book 3, the *pambasileus* is so superior because he has a kind of knowledge that no one else in the city has. But his knowledge of distributive justice, of political philosophy, so distinguishes him that, were he to receive his just deserts, all others in the city would be deprived of

121

political life. In democracy, articulating and acting on the principle
of the regime—freedom leading to equality—undermines the principle of the regime. And polity is actually constructed on the basis
of the regime's misunderstanding of itself. Books 7 and 8 are meant
to reconcile these two strands of the argument of the *Politics*: the
emphasis on the good or wisdom in Books 1–3 that culminates in
pambasileia and the emphasis on the just or freedom in Books 4–6
that culminates in democracy.

The instrument of this reconciliation is the beautiful—the *kalon*.
The regime that preserves itself because the good it aims at is education for the sake of something more than its own preservation
will be a regime where knowing and doing can be reconciled. In
the regime that takes itself seriously by not taking itself too seriously, the boundary between thoughts and deeds will blur. One might
also expect that in the discussion of this regime, the question of
the relation between the content of Aristotle's book—politics—and
its form—philosophy—might be resolved. It is no accident that Book
7 should begin with a discussion of the relation between the political life and the philosophical life.

> Concerning the best regime, it is necessary for him who intends
> to make the appropriate inquiry first to determine what is the
> life most to be chosen. For while this is unclear, the best regime
> is also necessarily unclear. For it is appropriate that those gov-
> erning themselves [being governed: *politeuomenous*] best (*arista*)
> given what exists for them, fare best [do the best things:
> *arista prattein*], if something does not happen contrary to reason.
> (1323a14–19)

This all looks fairly straightforward. Since the best regime is for
the sake of the best way of life, one cannot possibly know
what regime is best without determining what life is best. However, Aristotle's way of making the claim reveals a problem. If *po-
liteuomenous* is in the middle voice, it means something like
"governing themselves"; if passive, however, it might mean "being
governed."[96] There is a related ambiguity; the expression *arista
prattein* can be rendered as either "faring best" or "acting best"—
doing the best things. To fare well means to be satisfied with one's
life; to do good things need not mean that at all. Governing oneself
well has to do with knowing what one is doing; being governed
well implies nothing of the sort.

The best regime is the rule of the best. Rule by the wisest is clearly best insofar as it results in each citizen doing what is best for himself and for the whole city. The *pambasileus* rules like a father; the citizens are ruled. But the middle sense of the verb *politeuomai* has disappeared. To do the best things is not to fare well if one is thereby reduced to the status of a permanent child. This tension between freedom and order governs the final two books of the *Politics*. To what extent can faring best be reconciled with doing the best things?

Aristotle first asks "what life (*bios*) is most to be chosen, so to speak (*hôs eipein*), by all," and then indicates that much of what he will say about the best living (*zôê*) has already been said in what he calls here his external speeches (*exôterikoi logoi*). Aristotle's "so to speak" might well be rendered "so as to speak." The task is to use what has been said about living (*zôê*) in speeches that look at things from without in order to give an account adequate to our experience from within. The goal is not only "living," but living so as to speak—self-conscious living, or life (*bios*).[97] This interpretation of Aristotle's intent admittedly involves translating what are obviously secondary meanings as though they were primary. As long as we do not lose sight of the primary meanings, such a procedure is justified by what it brings to light.

If there are three sorts of goods—those external, those in the body, and those in the soul—clearly all three are required for faring well (1323a23–34). No matter how wealthy or attractive, a person in constant fear of death would live an unenviable life. Accordingly, courage is one of the goods of the soul without which nothing else can be altogether good. The virtues are necessary conditions for getting and keeping those external goods that are thought to contribute to happiness and so are good in the sense of being useful (*khrêsimon*).

This external account "through deeds" (*dia tôn ergôn*), according to which virtues are good, makes them seem means to a further end. Aristotle now introduces a second argument rooted not in deeds (*erga*) but in *logos*. External things are good only insofar as they are good *for* something—ultimately for some soul. The sign of this is that they have limits. There is never too much internal satisfaction with a good, but there is certainly such a thing as too much food. The good as the useful is therefore limited by that for which it is useful. Only that which is good for its own sake is without limit. Such a good is not useful but *kalon*—beautiful or noble. It is internal goods that are unlimited. And yet,

> generally it is clear, as we will assert, that the best disposition
> of each thing toward others with respect to preeminence follows
> the difference which it has received from the things of which we
> assert these themselves to be the dispositions. So that if the soul is
> more honorable than both possession and body, both simply and to
> us, the best disposition of each is necessarily analogous to these.
> Further, these things by nature are chosen for the sake of the soul,
> and all those who think well ought to choose them, but not soul for
> the sake of them. (1323b13–21)

If the body is to the soul as the goods of the body are to the goods
of the soul, and if the goods of the body are, as tools, necessarily
limited, while the goods of the soul are unlimited, then it follows
that the soul is unlimited. The soul is not a tool and so has no function external to itself. It cannot be understood as directed toward
anything outside itself. This seems to be what Aristotle means by
calling its goods *kalon*. But is this the human soul?

Aristotle first presents virtue as good in the sense of useful, then
in the sense of *kalon*. He now cites as an example a god, for whom
there is no necessity and so no external goods whatsoever, and who
is therefore happy and blessed "himself on account of himself." A
god, for whom there is no distinction between the good as useful
and the *kalon*, is never an instrument. Aristotle had claimed that
the soul was more honorable "both simply and to us." "To us" must
mean "to soul." Soul serves both as subject (that for whom things
are good) and as object (that which is good). Insofar as these two
are identical, the good as useful will be the same as the good as
kalon. But to the extent that what is good for soul is external, the
two will be different, and soul will be good for something. Human
beings differ from gods insofar as for us virtue must be understood
as double, as means to external goods that are then in turn necessary for internal satisfaction. Virtue is a composition of the *kalon*
on the one hand, and the *khrêsimon* (or, when understood in the
proper way, the good—the *agathon*) on the other. The virtuous man
is the *kalos k'agathos*—he who is beautiful and good. This doubleness is signaled by the city itself. Men are the purpose or end of
the regime—it is for the sake of their happiness, their faring best—
while at the same time, as citizens who perform functions in the
city, they are the means to that end—as tools they do the best things.
In the best regime these two must be one. The activity that preserves the city must somehow be that for which the city is preserved. This is of course easier to say than to do.

If the virtuous citizen is an instrument, his purpose is something like the happiness of the city as a whole. Aristotle is therefore forced to ask what the relation is between the happiness of the individual and the happiness of the city as a whole. He seems to finesse the issue.

> Whether the same happiness must be asserted to be both of each single human being and of the city or not the same, remains to say. But even this is apparent. For all would agree that it is the same. For whoever posit living well as wealth with respect to one person, these will also call the whole city blessed if it be wealthy, and whoever especially honor the tyrannical life, these would assert the city ruling the most men to be the happiest. And if someone allows the single man [to be happy] on account of virtue, he will also assert the more excellent (*spoudaioteran*) city to be the most happy. (1324a5–13)

All, of course, do not agree on what is good for the city; they agree, rather, that what they think good for themselves is also good for the city. What is the case in all cities is that *something* is honored. But even this does not overcome the tension between the happiness of the individual and that of the city. To pursue wealth as good is not the same as to wish to be honored for one's wealth. Only the latter requires a city in which wealth is celebrated. But to the extent that such a city pursues wealth itself, its citizens may have to subordinate their own pursuit of wealth and so sacrifice their own good as they understand it. Imperialism can be expensive. A citizen might donate a ship to the navy and be honored for doing something *kalon*, where the *kalon* has to do with supporting the city's overall purpose, its pursuit of wealth. But he would in fact be sacrificing his own wealth. Even when the city and man are understood to have a good in common, it is nevertheless not self-evident that the two goods will not conflict.

The real issue, however, is not the pursuit of wealth but philosophy. The life of contemplation stands as the model for the inner life par excellence—the life virtually independent because it requires so little from without. Consequently, Aristotle says two inquiries must be made: (1) whether the life most to be chosen is political or that of a stranger released (*apolelumenos*) from the political community and (2) what regime is best regardless of whether life in the political community is best for all or only for some. He justifies the second question as following from what we have in-

tentionally chosen (*proêirêmetha*)—political thought and contemplation. He then specifies that the alternative to the political or active
life is the life released (*apoleleumenos*) from everything external,
such as a contemplative life, which some assert to be the only
philosophic life. These are the two ways of life intentionally chosen (*proairoumenoi*) by those most ambitious with regard to
virtue. We need to notice in passing that Aristotle has stipulated his
own intentional choice—political philosophy—as a sort of hybrid
of the two.

If political virtue is instrumental virtue, the danger is that the
city in the name of which it is instrumental will also come to be
understood as instrumental. The man with instrumental virtue ex-
erts himself solely for the sake of what is external to him. When
the same understanding of virtue guides the city, it will define itself by its ability to extend its rule over others; it will become the
imperialistic city—the city at war. Aristotle's examples suggest that
this is the truth of all actual cities. The doubleness of virtue can
then be understood according to the following proportion: the internal : external :: philosophical : political :: nonimperialistic : imperialistic. As the best city must combine two sorts of virtue, the
internal and the external, it looks as though it has to combine elements of this proportion that are not obviously compatible. The best
city needs political virtue but must be nonimperialistic. Put somewhat differently, its citizens must practice political virtue, but it must
itself be modeled on philosophy.

Just as the city devoted to wealth need not contain wealthy men,
the city modeled on philosophy need not contain any philosophers.
In fact, it looks as though it would be hard for it to contain useful
parts that were themselves altogether independent of the larger
whole. Nevertheless, philosophy serves as the model for what Aristotle calls autotelic action.

> But it is not necessary that the active [life] be in relation to others,
> as some consider, nor that thinking alone to be active which comes
> to be from acting for the sake of the things which will result, but
> much more [are these active]: contemplations (*theôrias*) and thoughts
> (*dianoêseis*) which have their ends within themselves (*autoteleis*) and
> are for the sake of themselves. (1325b17–22)

The contemplative life is not passive, but active in the highest sense.
Its action, however, is not externally directed; it is instead characterized by internal motion. The city based on it will therefore be

active and at the same time self-contained. Accordingly, Aristotle
likens these two, the contemplative life and the best city, to the
cosmos; all three are *kalon*. Needless to say, just as it is hard to
place the autotelic contemplative within the autotelic city, it is hard
to understand either of them in their relation to the autotelic cosmos. How is it possible for a whole to be made up of parts that are
at the same time perfect wholes in their own rights? Aristotle's response to this question begins to emerge in his treatment of the parts
of the best regime in the remainder of Book 7.

The best regime may be autotelic, but, as the regime of a city, it
would have to confront certain necessities of nature. It would have
to be situated in a place, have a certain size, and have a certain
number of citizens, each of a particular age, sex, and character. And,
of course, there are tasks that must be performed for any city to
survive and yet more if it is to survive well. Aristotle acknowledges that the best regime must have equipment (1325b29) which, as
equipment, is not a product of the regime but must be present by
hypothesis. It is "what one would pray for," what is external to the
regime and makes it possible.

The number of parts of the city without which it cannot exist
is related to the number of necessary tasks (*erga*). Aristotle mentions six such tasks: sustenance, arts for the production of tools,
arms for both internal order and external defense, wealth, care for
the divine, and judgment with regard to the advantageous and
the just. It looks as though the parts of the city will follow
accordingly: farmers, artisans, soldiers, the rich, priests, and deliberators. Instead, Aristotle excludes artisans from citizenship because
their way of life is incompatible with virtue, which is after all
the goal of the regime (1328b34–41). And he not only excludes
farmers on the grounds that their lives lack the leisure necessary
for citizenship but indicates that what we pray for is that they will
be slaves (1330a26–27). The remaining four tasks are in fact ful-
filled by the same people, albeit at different times of their lives.
Those who own property are citizens. When young, they are soldiers, in middle age, they are deliberators, and as old men, priests.
Throughout the *Politics*, but especially in Books 4–6, the most
difficult problem has been what to do with the lower class, the
dêmos. Here in Book 7 Aristotle solves the problem by praying them
away. Those men absolutely necessary to the *polis* because they
produce its sustenance and its tools, who make its life possible, have
been transformed into tools. The *dêmos* seems to be the limit on

the combination of virtue as means with virtue as end in itself. Good farmers do not make good men.

Aristotle, of course, knows how problematic all this is. When he suggests that freedom be offered as a reward for slaves (1330a32–34), he tacitly admits that these cannot be the same as the slaves he previously argued to be so by nature. However, slavery for any but these is unjust, and so the best regime would seem to require either unjust slavery, and so imperfection in its deliberative element, or an ineducable demos, and so ignobility within its citizen body. Aristotle's "solution" here is obviously no solution at all. The *dêmos* represents an insurmountable obstacle to the coincidence of virtue as an end with virtue as means. But abolishing it in speech allows Aristotle to address those features of political life in which such a coincidence is possible.

What sort of citizen does the best regime require? People who rule themselves cannot be too malleable, but neither can they be too stubborn. Accordingly, Aristotle describes their natures as the proper mix of thinking and art with spirit (*thumos*). The *polis*, as we have seen, is a combination of order and freedom. Aristotle then goes on to say that in Europe men have an excess of *thumos* in relation to thought, while in Asia the disproportion is reversed. But

> the race of the Greeks, just as it is in the middle with respect to places, so it participates in both. . . . and the tribes of Greeks also have the same difference in relation to one another. (1327b29–34)

Thus, a difference in soul—an internal difference—is explained in terms of geography. Locate a city on the map, and you can read off the character of its citizen body. Later, and perhaps somewhat more plausibly, Aristotle presents a similar argument in terms of age. As to what the relation should be between those who are armed and those who deliberate, he remarks that they should be the same people but at different times of their lives since "by nature power is in the younger and prudence in the older" (1329a15–16), and

> nature has given the distinction, making what is the same with respect to the same genus (*genos*) now younger and now older, of which to the one being ruled is appropriate and to the other ruling. (1332b36–39).

The old are thus by nature more suitable to rule than the young.

What all of this means becomes clearer when Aristotle discusses the physical characteristics of the best city. It must be both near the sea, since it does need external trade, and away from the sea, since it is to be to the greatest extent possible autotelic. This double demand will be physically satisfied by establishing a port area separated off from the city proper (1327a30–39). Later Aristotle makes a similar distinction with respect to ownership of the land (1330a9–20). Reflecting the split between the whole and its parts, Aristotle divides the land first into a common part and privately owned parts. The common part is then further divided into a part that treats the city's needs as a whole (the part concerned with meeting needs of services to the gods) and a part that serves the public needs insofar as it is used by citizens severally (for example, providing for common messes). Each privately owned part is then also divided in two, with a part near the center of the city and a part on the periphery. The goal is to make each citizen reproduce in himself those external differences in the city that might lead to differing assessments of the good of the whole. During an invasion in an ordinary city, those with land near the borders will be inclined to want immediate action to be taken to defend their homes, while those with property only in the heart of the city will be inclined to wait to see what happens. In this city each citizen will feel both inclinations. Everyone is simultaneously from upstate and downstate.

Perhaps most revealing is Aristotle's description of where the city should be located. For purposes of health and defense, it is to be on a slope. The locations of fortified places will vary depending on the regime. Monarchy and oligarchy fortify a height—an acropolis—democracy occupies level places, and aristocracy has a number of strong places. As to walls, Aristotle is quite clear: you need them. While there is something to the old-fashioned view that it is more *kalon* to defend the city with men, a city can always choose to ignore its walls, but a city without walls cannot suddenly choose to have them when it is outnumbered. Walls are an artifice fulfilling Aristotle's earlier "prayer" that the city be located in a place easy of exit but difficult of access. He adds that these walls

> must be cared for in order that with respect to the city they may hold suitably both in relation to order [or ornament: *kosmon*] and in relation to the needs of war. (1331a12–14)

That walls are to be both ornamental and useful points to what is most striking about the physical ordering (*diakosmeô*—1331a23) of the best city. The houses given over to the gods and those where the rulers have common meals are highest on the slope of this city, although, significantly, not on the top. Their location has a double justification.

> And the place would be such [i.e., suitable] if it is suffi-
> ciently conspicuous in relation to its position and in relation to the
> neighboring parts of the city more fortified. (1331a28–31)

Farther down the hill is what is called a free market, which is purged of all merchandise and purged as well of all the nonfree members of the city—artisans and farmers. Here free men are at leisure, whereas in the commercial market further down the slope, necessities are dealt with.

Now this external arrangement of things on a slope is interesting because it corresponds perfectly to the internal hierarchy of the city itself. This is a city in which the "higher things" are really physically higher and in which necessities are simultaneously adornments. Aristotle excludes the *dêmos* as most recalcitrant to this sort of coincidence and then transforms the city into a place where nothing is accidental. It becomes a poem in which the parts seem at first as haphazard as the events of real life but in the end fit together like a book. Aristotle has made a city in which all things external and bodily—geography, age, place, property, even the walls of the city—are really images for other things. To be sure, body and externality are present, but they have lost their defining features as limits on the autotelic character of political life. These bodies will not require guarding.[98] They are like the bodies in books—Oedipus' swollen feet or Ahab's missing leg. As all the details of the city are now meaningful, no private good or preference could be irrelevant. That is, when all difference is of generalizable significance, the split between the public and the private disappears. This city, where nothing occurs contrary to reason (*paralogon*—1323a19), where necessities are ornaments, is the city that one would pray for.

It is only in a political order of this sort that the distinction between the good as useful and the good as *kalon* could be overcome.[99] If my ownership of land is not only necessary for the existence of the city but structured in such a way that it is symbolic of the very being of the city, then owning it is not only a means to an end;

ownership somehow embodies the end to which it is a means. When the walls of the city are not only necessary for protection but are also an image of that which they are protecting, then building them is not simply a means to an end but a celebration of the end itself. When I open my eyes and see not only where things are, but in seeing where they are see also what they are, then the objects around me become not only things utilized by the city, but the city itself.

Aristotle is not the first to have seen this point. In Plato's *Laws* the Athenian Stranger proposes the following response to the poets who wish to be admitted to the regime being founded.

> Best of strangers, we ourselves to the greatest extent possible are the poets of a tragedy at once the most beautiful and best. At least, all our regime has put together an imitation of the most beautiful and best life, which we say really to be the truest tragedy. (817b)

The best political order requires men in two ways; as ends their virtue is *kalon*, as means it is *khrêsimon*. To succeed completely the best regime would have to make this double virtue one. The same activity would have to be both for itself and for some external or exoteric end. The exoteric becomes esoteric when it becomes symbolic. The best regime therefore must be a poem, making meaningful what is dictated by necessity but is otherwise meaningless. When in the *Poetics* (1451b5–11) Aristotle remarks that poetry is something more philosophic than is history, he means that, while both seem to deal with particular events, this is something of an illusion in poetry, the very being of which is to make generally significant what is on its face particular and insignificant. Only in a regime that is like a poem can the tension between the good of the part and the good of the whole be resolved. Insofar as it is possible not only to serve the whole but in the very same action to embody the whole one serves, it will be possible for the man who does the best things to fare the best. By articulating what is beautiful or noble within the sphere of the necessary, poetry makes political life possible. Poetic education is therefore the necessary feature of political life. Accordingly, Aristotle considers it in some detail in the final book of the *Politics*.

Chapter Eight

Poetry and Politics:
Politics Book 8

Book 7 prepares us for the importance of education to the best regime, but we still wonder at the extended treatment of music and poetry in Book 8. At first glance, it is certainly odd that a hard-nosed book about politics marches us to the conclusion that music is the goal of political life. Perhaps we need a second glance.

By arguing that the pursuit of the necessities of life can in the best regime be made coincident with the pursuit of the *kalon*, Book 7 seems to lead to the happy conclusion that political virtue, which is a means to an end, can be reconciled with that virtue which is an end in itself—philosophical virtue. The good life and the means to the good life consist in the same activity. Book 8, less sanguine, seems to argue that esoteric philosophic virtue depends on exoteric political virtue. If Book 7 tells us that building the city's walls can be satisfying for its own sake, Book 8 tells us that poetry and music cannot be understood other than as reflections on building walls; they are beautiful reflections on the useful. Were the city itself the perfect poem—the coincidence of the beautiful and the useful—then poetry would not need to be taught within the city.

The argument about education concerns, first of all, whether it is education of thinking or of character and, second, whether it should be directed at the useful, at virtue, or at what Aristotle calls here extraordinary or odd things (*ta peritta*). It looks as though education of character means education to virtue. Education of thinking clearly has to do with the useful, as Aristotle's subsequent account indicates. At *ta peritta* we are left to wonder. The sequel makes clear that while of course one must learn certain things for the sake of others, and so education will of necessity be to some extent concerned with the useful, its ultimate goal is virtue understood as autotelic activity. On the level of the individual, Aristotle gives that activity the name *skholê*, leisure. Education to the useful is permissible only to the extent that it is not at cross-purposes with the primary goal of education, virtue. Hence, the young are not to be educated in anything that will make them vulgar (*banauson*). Aristotle then says that he means by a banausic or vulgar deed or art "whatever renders either the body, soul, or thinking of the free useless with respect to the uses and actions of virtue" (1337b8–12).[100] This warning against the useful goes so far as to include the "free sciences" when they become too concerned with precision. Leisure is to be the goal of education because virtuous, or autotelic, action is the goal of the best regime. Music, the model for such action, is good because it is useless.

Aristotle's examples of what he has in mind are odd, however. He quotes two passages from the *Odyssey*.[101] In the first, the swineherd Eumaeus is defending Odysseus who, disguised as a beggar, is sitting at table with Penelope's suitors and listening to a singer. Odysseus, of course, is plotting to kill them. This musical activity of free men at leisure is in fact a disguise for utilitarian activity of a rather brutal kind. In the second quotation Odysseus himself speaks. He is at a banquet at the house of Alcinous in Phaeacia; the song he praises, which has constituted their leisure, is an account of the Trojan War. Is that what leisure consists in, listening to songs about war? In both of these instances, leisure proves parasitical upon lack of leisure. Contrary to initial appearances, it is leisure, *skholê*, which is the negation of lack of leisure, *askholia*.[102] Music, which was introduced as free and *kalon* and which is now distinguished even from political activity, requires the slavish and ugly to be what it is. This is perhaps more manifest in epic poetry, but, if Aristotle is correct about the manner in which musical mode can render human mood—about the way music directly represents what is in the soul—it is clear that the beauty of a musical representation of, for example, anger would require the existence of anger and so of things to get angry about. What is done for its own sake seems always to consist in a reflection on what is done for the sake of something else. The reflection may be autotelic, but it exists only as a sort of supervention on action that is heterotelic. Those fare best (*arista prattein*), and so are happy, who in leisure reflect apparently unselfconsciously on doing the best things (*arista prattein*) in the face of adversity.

In Book 8 this problem repeatedly takes the form of the question of whether education in music requires that one learn to play an instrument. That is, is it important that one become an instrument for one's own leisure activity? On the one hand, to play an instrument means to acknowledge necessity. On the other hand, something like acknowledging necessity is a condition for understanding and appreciating music. To ask how much one should play, then, amounts to asking how much one should acknowledge necessity. In the midst of asking this question, Aristotle introduces a second issue.

> At the same time, children must (*dei*) have some pastime, and the rattle of Archytus, which they give to children in order that, using it, they will break none of the things of the household, [must] be considered to have come to be beautifully. (1340b26–29)

This rattle (invented by a philosopher) is given to children so they won't break the things of the household. Music, then, keeps us from breaking up the home; it substitutes simulated motion for real motion. The sentence itself is revealing. The necessity for children to have some pastime and the necessity to consider this pastime to have come to be beautifully are expressed by one and the same word, *dei*. The two are quite literally the same necessity. Music and poetry can have such power because thinking and moving, while admittedly different, are governed by the same necessity. The education of Book 8 is, therefore, double; it may be directed either toward the useful or toward the *kalon*, but, like the virtuous actions of Book 7, it is nevertheless one education.

The music and poetry, on which the city depends, have the power to appeal to men in a twofold way. Our actions must simultaneously be understood as autotelic and as directed toward external goods. That the exoteric admits of being read esoterically provides a problematic unity to this dyad. Still, a difficulty remains. Aristotle began Book 8 with the suggestion that there are *three* competing understandings of the purpose of education; virtue, the useful, and *ta peritta*—the odd or outstanding things. The expression is used sparingly but in interesting ways in the *Politics*. It appears thrice in

Book 2, once referring admiringly to the speeches of Socrates (1265a12), once not so admiringly to the way of life of Hippodamus—the first man to give an account of the best regime (1267b22), and once to the way the Carthaginians govern themselves in comparison to others (1272b24–26). *Ta peritta* come up again in Book 8 in the discussion of how to avoid vulgarity in education. Aristotle indicates that the young should not toil too long at those works that are wondrous and outstanding or odd (*ta thaumasia kai peritta*). There seem, then, to be connections on the one hand between philosophy and *ta peritta* and on the other between banausic, or vulgar, and *ta peritta*. Aristotle nudges us to a conclusion by saying that it is as vulgar to master sciences completely as it is to master instruments and then referring us to the philosophers for precise speech (*akribologia*) about which musical modes have which effects (1341b26ff). Philosophy is vulgar.

The best political order is one where the good man is happy and is a good citizen. He can fulfill his function as part while reaping his satisfaction as a whole. For that to be possible, the distinction between virtue as a means and virtue as an end in itself must be blurred. Music, and finally poetry, accomplish this end. They are also suited to many other ends, however, and can corrupt as easily as educate. Consequently, in the best regime they need to be regulated. Someone would have to be aware of the symbolic import of the location of the free *agora* in order for it not to be relocated for apparently sensible and utilitarian reasons. (One might say the same of the Electoral College.) But to be aware of this symbolism is no longer to be enchanted by it in the same way. The last book of the *Politics* is notable for having introduced censorship without having described how the censors are to be educated. Aristotle began Book 7 by saying what the actions of the legislator must be, but never does he indicate that these are actions that the legislator does for their own sakes. The education of the legislators would require a reflection on the connection between the useful and the *kalon* which, in revealing the political utility of the *kalon*, would (to stretch a point) render it ugly. Because, even at this high level, knowing the good is at odds with doing the good, for the rational animal, doing the good is not simply good.

The coincidence of the autotelic and the useful, of the philosophic and the political, in Book 7 is therefore something of a myth. We knew that already, given the prayerful disposal of the *dêmos* in the best regime. But a third sort of education is mentioned in Book 8. Education directed toward *ta peritta* is on the surface akin to education directed at vulgar utility. At the same time, as a reflection on the relation between the useful and the *kalon*, it is both useful (necessary for censorship) and autotelic and so in its way *kalon*. At one point in Book 8 Aristotle calls what he is doing a prelude to the tune (*endosimos*—1339a13) of the speeches that will follow. He thereby indicates the "musical" character of his own work. The true coincidence of the useful and the *kalon* is not a philosophical politics, but perhaps it is political philosophy (at 1265a11 Socrates' *logoi* were described as possessing the *peritton*). If the relation between the useful and the *kalon* is the same as the relation between the external and the internal, the exoteric and the esoteric (1323b25), this would go a long way toward accounting for Aristotle's mode of writing in the *Politics*. His book would mirror in its form the problem at the core of the city. This problem is not adventitious. The political being is the being with *logos*, about whom one can say that he "by nature desires to be in a state of knowing" (*Metaphysics* 980a22) and yet for whom the fundamental question "is now and will always be sought and always be perplexing" (*Metaphysics* 1028b2–4). The apparently unfinished state of the *Politics* is a reflection of the fact that wonder is in some sense both the beginning and the end of philosophy.[103]

Notes

1. In the *Poetics* (1457b3–6) Aristotle uses the word for sovereign, *kuri-on*, to describe what turns out to be one of two fundamental aspects of all *logos*—the ordinary. It is paired with the foreign. See also my *Aristotle's Poetics: The Poetry of Philosophy* (Savage, Md.: Rowman and Littlefield, 1992), 111–28.

2. This dyad is connected to a variety of others. In Book 1 it will underlie the division of the household into slave and free, the double treatment of nature as teleological, and the double account of the art of acquisition. In Book 2 it will be at the root of the tension between political knowledge and political practice. In Book 3 it shows itself as the tension between poverty and wealth that ultimately leads to the tensions between the rule of law and the rule of the *pambasileus*—the all-powerful king—and between philosophy as a model for political life and philosophy as an element of political life. In Books 4 and 6 the dyad is connected to oligarchy and democracy as the elements of all political life, and in Book 5 to the negative determination of the *polis*. In Books 7–8 it is linked to the double accounts of virtue and of education. The list could easily be extended. To see how far-reaching the implications are of the distinction made at the outset of the *Politics*, one need only mention the similar dualism in the *Metaphysics*, where a comprehensive or "democratic" understanding of "being as being" is played off against a hierarchical account of being as the highest being.

3. See Plato's *Phaedrus* 230d.

4. Compare 1324b39–1325a1: ". . . just as one ought not hunt human beings for a feast or a sacrifice but what is to be hunted for this, and whatever wild animal may be eaten is to be hunted."

5. Compare the beginning of Book 8 (1338b20–30) on cannibalism and murder as the signs of barbarism and also *Nicomachean Ethics* 1143b20–25.

6. Compare *Nicomachean Ethics* 1161a31–b11 where Aristotle makes clear that neither friendship nor justice is possible between master and slave.

7. Aristotle nevertheless hints at what is to come in the examples that accompany the first statement of nature as teleological. It is curious that he mentions three natural classes to which we are meant to compare the *polis*: man, horse, and household (*oikia*). We are led to wonder whether men are

139

like horses, presumably ends in themselves, or like households, which cannot be what they are apart from their completion in cities.

8. Compare Book 3 (1288a25–30) on the *pambasileus* understood as the whole of which the other citizens are parts.

9. Compare this with the critique of Plato in Book 2, especially 1261a17–21.

10. That Aristotle is aware of this difficulty even in the *Nicomachean Ethics* becomes clear if one considers the manner in which the multiplicity of goods suggested by the first part of the first sentence of the book is undermined by the introduction of "the good" in the second part of the sentence. The good becomes the *ergon* of the goods, and they thereby cease to be *energeiai*.

11. Compare 1252a18.

12. The first sentence of every book of the *Politics* after Book 1 contains the word *politeia*. See Leo Strauss, *The City and Man* (Chicago: Rand McNally, 1964), 45.

13. This repeated division into three is made clear in Harry V. Jaffa's analysis of Book 2 of the *Politics* (although he does not make its significance explicit) in his "Aristotle" in Leo Strauss and Joseph Cropsey, eds., *History of Political Philosophy* (Chicago: Rand McNally, 1963, 1972), 80–94.

14. See Aristotle's *De Caelo* 268a8–29 and Strauss, *The City and Man*, 17–22.

15. See Strauss, *The City and Man*, 18.

16. See Strauss, *The City and Man*, 22.

17. Aristotle divides the objects of desire into three—the necessary, the superfluous, and pure pleasure unmixed with pain. *Stasis* can arise from any of the three. The cure for the first is a minimum amount of property and work, for the second moderation, and for the third philosophy.

18. This is confirmed by Aristotle's use of *idion* and words cognate with it in Chapter 12.

19. See, for example, *Nicomachean Ethics* 1099a31–b8.

20. There is an additional wrinkle in the division. Aristotle divides each of the last two categories into two. So they either legislate (or legislate and craft a regime) in their own cities or in foreign cities. At the very least what Aristotle has done is to make it impossible to consider his final division a straightforward division into three. Is this his escape from the mistake of Hippodamus?

21. See note 17 above.

22. See 1274b33–35 and 1276a5–b15.

23. "For they dispute, some saying the city to have done [acted] a deed [action], but some [saying] not the city but the oligarchy or the tyranny." (1274b33–35)

24. Forms of *aporia, aporos,* and *aporeô* occur at least twenty-nine times in Book 3.

25. "But we see that all the activity (*pragmateia*) of the statesman (*politikos*) and of the legislator is about the city, and the regime is an order of

those making the city their home. But since a city is one of the composite things, like any other whole put together and from many parts, it is clear that the citizen must first be sought." (1274b35–40)

26. Book 3, as a whole, has the following structure:

1. Introduction: chapter 1 (1274b32–1275a1)
2. Who are the citizens?: chapters 1–2 (1275a1–1276a5)
3. When is a city the same?: chapter 3
4. The extremes of citizenship:
   a. Good men—chapter 4
   b. The vulgar/slaves/etc.—chapter 5
5. The forms of regime: chapters 6–8
6. Various illegitimate claims to rule based on misunderstandings of justice, or the deviant regimes: chapters 9–11
7. Justice: chapter 12
8. Legitimate claims: chapter 13
9. Kingship as the hardest case: chapters 14–18

27. This is connected to the distinction present in the language of Aristotle's argument between what is said and what is true. See, for example, 1275a28–30, 33, 1275b3, 18, 1276a3, 6, and 15, although it must be said that this sort of language is very common for Aristotle.

28. Compare 1313a14–16.

29. Compare this with Glaucon's demand at the beginning of Book 2 of the *Republic* that justice be good, independent of appearances. Socrates responds first by setting up a city in which there is no distinction between appearance and reality and then, once this city has been corrupted, by trying to restore it to health by closing the gap between appearance and reality. Aristotle too sees that this claim to close the gap between what things are and what they are called is the paradigm for all politics. In neither case, of course, does this mean that they think such a restoration is really possible.

30. *Nicomachean Ethics* 1277b30.

31. Aristotle elsewhere denies the special status of oligarchy and democracy, although it is interesting that he devotes so much attention to both in Book 4 and especially to democracy in Book 6.

32. "And indeed, what has been sought in the past and now and ever, and what is always puzzling (*aporoumenon*)—What is being (*on*)?—is this: What is substance (*ousia*)?" *Metaphysics* 1128b2–6.

33. In Book 3, at least, oligarchy is sometimes allowed to stand for hierarchical rule of any sort. See, for example, 1281a30–34.

34. Aristotle uses a peculiar analogy to bring out the incompleteness.

But, of men, those who are good differ from each of the many in this (just as they also say the beautiful [differ from] the not beautiful and things painted/written through art [differ from] true things), in combining things scattered and apart into one, since, having been set apart, the eye belonging to this man is more beautiful than the painted one, and another part than some other. (1281b10–16)

Thus, the good man : one of the many :: beautiful : not beautiful :: things painted/written by art : true things :: one : scattered. The eye of a real person may be more beautiful, but it will not be more beautiful as part of a whole. True things therefore do not really fit into wholes and are in this respect "not beautiful." The suggestion seems to be that there is some truth to the democratic claims, but this truth is not compatible with the beautiful or noble actions that are the goal of political life (1281a1–3).

35. At *Nicomachean Ethics* 1152a36 Aristotle does mention "the one philosophizing with respect to the political" (*tou tēn politikēn philosophountos*) in connection with the contemplation of pleasure and pain.

36. Democracy awards the same to all regardless of merit, taking the genuine equality of men in one respect to be equality in all respects. Oligarchy treats one inequality, wealth, as though it meant that men were unequal in all respects. Both narrow the purpose of the city. Oligarchy treats it as though it were a corporation—the number of shares you own determines your influence. Democracy treats it as though it were simply a self-defense league—everyone is equally able to bear arms. But as the city has as its goal the good life for its citizens, and as it is possible to be both rich and unhappy and free and unhappy, neither democracy nor oligarchy properly understands the city.

37. Consider, for example, Herodotus' *Inquiries* 3.76 with the first note in Rousseau's *Second Discourse*.

38. "For surely they would not say such a man should be expelled and banished, nor indeed should such a man be ruled. For it would be almost as if, by dividing offices, they should claim to rule over Zeus." (1286b28–31)

39. See 1284a3–15.

40. See Aristophanes, *Frogs* 1431–32 and Plato, *Phaedo* 99c–102a.

41. Aristotle claims to distinguish Spartan kingship from heroic kingship. One would think that Agamemnon would serve as an example of the latter. However, Aristotle uses him as an example of the limited powers belonging to kings who are primarily commanders. He cites the *Iliad* to show that Agamemnon had life-and-death authority over his troops but, as a king at home, did not necessarily have such authority (1285a11–12). Several things are curious here. First, the verse in which Agamemnon claims this authority ("For death is in my power.") is not in our versions of the *Iliad*. Second, in the context (*Iliad* 391–393), the way Agamemnon is forced to use persuasion to rally his troops indicates that death is not simply in his power. Finally, it is curious to restrict Agamemnon's life-or-death authority to war when the war began only after he ordered the sacrifice of his daughter Iphigeneia.

42. What is true of the good city is also true of the virtuous man, who must somehow combine aiming at and being at the mean (*Nicomachean Ethics* 1106b27-28).

43. See, for example 1276a23, 1277b36, 1278b1, 1284a8, and especially 1281a3. For the legal use of *theteon* as "it is to be established or set down," see Plato, *Laws* 832e.

44. For an account of the dispute see Carnes Lord, *Aristotle: The Politics* (Chicago: University of Chicago Press, 1984) 15–17.

45. See Ernest Barker, *The Politics of Aristotle* (New York: Oxford University Press, 1962) xxxix–xli, 152–53 and 279; Carnes Lord, *Aristotle: The Politics* (Chicago: University of Chicago Press, 1984) 15–17, 117 and 197; H. Rackham, *Aristotle*: Politics (Cambridge, Mass.: Loeb Classical Library, 1972) 274–75 and 532–33; *Politica* translated by Benjamin Jowett in *The Basic Works of Aristotle* (New York: Random House, 1966) 1205, 1277; T.A. Sinclair, *Aristotle: The Politics* (New York: Penguin Classics, 1978) 148 and 255.

46. *anagkê dê ton mellonta peri autês poiêsasthai tên prosêkousan skêpsin* in Book 3 and *peri politeias aristês ton mellonta poiêsasthai tên prosêkousan zêtêsin anagkê diorisasthai prôton tis hairetôtatos bios* in Book 7.

47. Compare Plato's *Symposium* 205b–c.

48. This is the mirror image of the problem central to Book 1, where the complete triumph of the good—the strong teleology—led to a situation in which citizens did the good without willing to do the good. Without justice, doing the good is simply high-level slavery. See chapter 1 above.

49. Compare 1318b6–1319a20.

50. See *Nicomachean Ethics* 1094a19–b12.

51. See 1252a1–8.

52. Accordingly, to identify the *eidos* of one's *polis* is to give it a *genos*.

53. See especially 1289a32–34.

54. Accordingly, compare *Nicomachean Ethics* 1094a with *Metaphysics* 982b.

55. Once again, see *Nicomachean Ethics* 1094a and *Metaphysics* 982b as well as 1026a.

56. See Seth Benardete, "On Wisdom and Philosophy: The First Two Chapters of Aristotle's *Metaphysics* A," *Review of Metaphysics* (1978): 205–15 and my "The End of Final Causality: Aristotle's *Metaphysics* A" (forthcoming).

57. See *Nicomachean Ethics* 1094a–b.

58. Curiously, Aristotle says that to contemplate the best *politeia* is the same as to speak about these terms—*onomata* (1289a32–34). The emphasis on speaking the name of the regime to make it an object of contemplation suggests again that the being of the *politeia* has fundamentally to do with its being perceived.

59. "It remains for us to speak about tyranny, not that much can be said about it, but in order that it may take its part in the inquiry, since we set it down as a part of the regimes." (1295a1–3)

60. It is probably no accident that democracy and oligarchy are the first regimes to appear in Book 4 (1289a20–25). Consider, for example, how they are singled out at 1289a18–22.

61. Compare Plato's *Republic* 344d–347a with 369e–370c.

62. Compare 1291a17–19.

63. See *Republic* 474b; Strauss, *The City and Man*, 78–80, 94–97, 122–24; and Seth Benardete, *Socrates' Second Sailing* (Chicago and London: University of Chicago Press, 1989), 20–32, 44–54, 123–29.

64. Compare 1289a28.

65. See also *Republic* 399a–c.

66. Perhaps Aristotle's criticism of the *Republic* is also meant to indicate that he too cannot be slavish while doing what he is doing.

67. See Aristotle's *De Anima* 413b.

68. See chapter 3 above.

69. One must recall that for Aristotle *politeia* means both "regime" and a fifth form of regime in addition to the four ordinarily mentioned. Plato omitted this form in particular in his book, *Politeia*, or *Republic* (1293a38–b1).

70. It is not simply coincidence that it is also the nature of philosophy that to discuss it means to discuss it as something else. Thinking is always thinking something, and the something that is thought affects the character of the act of thinking it. See Aristotle's *Metaphysics* Z.17 and L.1.

71. For a very rich and much fuller interpretation of this section of Book 4 see Harvey C. Mansfield, *Taming the Prince* (New York and London: Free Press, 1989), 45-71.

72. See 1313a38–b6.

73. Consider also Aristotle's two lists of the general causes of revolution in chapters 2 and 3 and the prominence of gain (*kerdos*), hybris, and honor (*timê*).

74. Accordingly, democracy seems to be still more fundamental than oligarchy, which in its way admits of being understood as democratic. Wealth is a popular understanding of what sets the few apart from the many (1302a1–2). It is a quantitative measure of a qualitative difference and so betrays a strangely democratic understanding of the unit of measurement (1301b30–35). The priority of the *dêmos* can be seen in yet another way. Since there are various ways in which the few can be few, in oligarchies it is possible for faction to arise within the ruling class, but the *dêmos* can never choose a different *dêmos* (1302a7–13). It is in this sense more truly the city than any few who rule. Accordingly, Aristotle tends to refer to the two fundamental forms of regime as oligarchy and, instead of democracy, the *dêmos* (for example, at 1301b39).

75. Because *metabolê* in its political sense does mean fundamental change, it is hard to avoid translating it by revolution. Yet revolution as we know it is almost impossible to separate in thought from *the* revolution. Not even our home-grown war of independence has the intellectual power for us of the French Revolution of 1789. Every major intellectual figure of the nineteenth century, the foundation of our own century, seems to have been forced in one way or another to come to terms with it. Aristotle, of course, has nothing to say about the French Revolution. It is hard to imagine how to think about modern revolution without thinking about the modern nation-state, progress,

Notes 145

ideology, history, and mass movements. It is hard to understand Aristotle without avoiding these terms.

76. Ernest Barker, *The Politics of Aristotle* (New York: Oxford University Press, 1962), 242.

77. See *Physics* 192b21–23 and *Metaphysics* 1025b19–22.

78. Even the language used reflects the importance of chance in the argument. The verb *sumbainô*, to happen, a form of which, *sumbebêkos*, is Aristotle's standard word for the accidental (see, for example, *Metaphysics* 1025a30–34), increases markedly in frequency in Book 5. It occurs in various forms at least twenty-eight times: 1302a4, 1303a3, 1303a10, 1303a31, 1303b20, 1303b33, 1304b20, 1304b39, 1305b5–6, 1305b33, 1306a9, 1306b27, 1306b37, 1307a27, 1307b22, 1308a36, 1308b8, 1309a7, 1309a39, 1309b30, 1310b1–2, 1310b14, 1311a18, 1312a38, 1312b29, 1312b40, and 1313b27–79. The verb more or less drops out when Aristotle begins his account of how to preserve tyranny.

79. While it would not be correct to say that the argument of Book 5 forces the reader to turn to Plato's *Symposium*, and specifically to Aristophanes' speech, there are certain parallels between the two texts that make it easy for the *Symposium* to come to mind here. Aristotle mentions the name "Pausanias" thrice (1301b20–21, 1307a4, and 1311b2), admittedly referring to men other, and in the first two cases much more famous than, the character in the *Symposium*. Nevertheless, they serve to remind one of the dialogue. He cites the attack on the sons of Peisistratus (Hipparchus, the Athenian tyrant, and Hippias, his brother) by Harmodius and Aristogeiton (1311a34–39) as one of his examples of tyrannicide. It is a major example in the *Symposium* in the speech of Pausanias (180c–185e). Since the *Symposium* is the Platonic dialogue most clearly and completely devoted to *erôs*, it is perhaps not surprising that so many of the issues in it should be present in Book 5, where Aristotle is preoccupied with *erôs*—issues such as pederasty, hybris, and castration. Finally, that Aristotle is aware that what appears to be Plato's least political dialogue in fact has a great deal to do with politics is clear from his reference to the *Symposium* at *Politics* 1262b10–14, where he uses Aristophanes' speech to call into question the view presented in the *Republic* that the goal of the best regime is the greatest possible unity.

80. This account of Aristophanes' speech relies heavily on the interpretation of Leo Strauss presented in a course given on the *Symposium* at the University of Chicago (transcription, no date). See also my *Ancient Tragedy and the Origins of Modern Science* (Carbondale: Southern Illinois University Press, 1988) 5–13.

81. See, for example, *Meno* 73c–d and 86d–e, as well as *Gorgias* 452d.

82. The word for castration, *hê ektomê*, is related to the words used to describe the "cutting" or castration of the circle-men by Zeus (temô, diatemô, hê tomê, etc. *Symposium*, 190d–e).

83. This is why we find the American Revolution so little revolutionary. It is also what makes it so worthy of study. We have become more accustomed to revolutionary rhetoric of the following sort.

> Communism as *positive* overcoming [*Aufhebung*] of *private property* as
> *human self-alienation*, and therefore as real *appropriation* of *human*
> essence through and for human beings; therefore as a return—complete,
> conscious, and coming to be within the whole wealth of development
> heretofore—of human beings for themselves as *social*, i.e., human, be-
> ings. This communism is as consummate naturalism equal to human-
> ism, and as consummate humanism equal to naturalism; it is the true
> resolution of the conflict of human beings with nature, and with human
> beings, the true resolution of the conflict between existence and es-
> sence, between objectification and self-confirmation, between freedom
> and necessity, between individual and species. It is the riddle of history
> solved and knows itself as this solution. [Karl Marx, Werke, Schriften
> bis 1844, Erster Teil Ergänzungsband (Berlin, 1968) 536—the transla-
> tion is my own]

Marx understood very well what sort of radical change would be required in
order for a revolution of the final sort to be achieved. Nothing short of a
transformation of human nature as it had hitherto shown itself would be necessary for revolution to be more than a change of one regime into another—
sometimes justifiable, sometimes not, but always impermanent and imperfect.
A change of regimes can become revolutionary in the modern sense only when
stasis means something different from *metabolê*.

84. See Plato's *Timaeus* 19a–20c and *Republic* 466d–e.

85. Perhaps this is what it means to say that the *polis* originates by nature
in the household. We are born into a situation where we are already ruled. In
the language of Plato's Aristophanes, we were whole—circle-men—only before we were born. Being born means being cut down the middle. The original circle-men are pregnant women, and politics is a kind of parricide.

86. Compare Rousseau's *Discours sur l'origine et les fondements de
l'inégalité parmi les hommes*, vol. 2 of *Oeuvres Complètes* (Paris: Editions
du Seuil, 1971), 233-34.

87. See, for example, Lord, 265, note 2 and Rackham, 484, note e.

88. See, for example, Lord, 266, note 31 and Barker, 278, note 2.

89. See, for example, 1290b1, 1294a12, and 1304b31 to cite only a few
cases.

90. In this way, its movement parallels the movement of the last of the
books of the first part of the *Politics*, Book 3, which begins with individual
citizens as the stuff out of which cities are formed and ends with the absolute rule of the single best man—the *pambasileus*—who is in a way the only
true citizen. Like Book 6, Book 3 moves from the demands of equality and
freedom to the demands of hierarchy and rule.

91. See chapter 2 above.

92. See Mary Nichols, *Citizens and Statesmen: A Study of Aristotle's* Politics (Savage, Md: Rowman and Littlefield, 1992), 117–18 and John C. Cal-
houn, *A Disquisition on Government* (Indianapolis and New York: Bobbs-
Merrill, 1953) 19–44.

93. See chapter 3 above.

94. The gods emerge here as a check on the tyrannical impulses of the *dêmos*; the more a regime departs from the just, the more it must rely on the sacred as a substitute.

95. This tension is connected to the split between moral and intellectual virtue in the *Nicomachean Ethics*.

96. *Politeumai* regularly has the passive sense of "to be governed" in the sense of a city being governed (see, for example, *Republic* 427a). In the middle voice it can have the active sense of living as a free citizen or taking part in government. This of course comes very close to meaning that one governs oneself. Such a meaning is certainly at least latently present in its form and in certain passages seems to be more than that. Consider, for example, the first sentence of the *Education of Cyrus*, where Xenophon reflects on how many democracies have been dissolved "by those somehow otherwise wishing to be governed (*politeuesthai*) rather than in a democracy." Surely if *they* dissolve the democracy, they somehow wish to govern themselves differently. Since nothing in the form requires that it be read as a passive rather than a middle, this passage too is ambiguous.

97. See 1253a15–16 and chapter 1 above.

98. See chapter 6 above.

99. See, for example, 1332b36–42 where Aristotle makes it clear that only those who think of themselves as eventually being rulers will be willing to act in a subordinate capacity now. Doing what has to be done—the necessary things—is understood as a means to a future end.

100. It looks as though there is a suppressed standard of utility here, perhaps what is useful for the regime.

101. With the exception of the quotation about the cyclops in Book 1, all of the previous quotations from Homer in the *Politics* are from the *Iliad*, the poem about war. Predictably enough, the quotations here are from the *Odyssey*, the peace poem.

102. This may have something to do with the increased frequency with which Aristotle uses double negations to describe what he is doing in Book 8, e.g., 1337b5, 16, 20; 1339a27; 1340b22.

103. See my "The End of Final Causality: Aristotle's *Metaphysics* A," (forthcoming).

Index

acquisition, art of. *See khrêmatistikê*
agathon, 124
anger, 96, 99
aporia, 45–48, 52–53, 55–56, 58–61, 80–81, 110, 121–22, 140n24
arista prattein, 122, 135
aristocracy, 10, 42, 52, 68, 74, 82
Aristophanes, 93–96, 110, 145n79, 145n80
Aristotle, 42, 126; *Metaphysics*, xi–xii, 72, 137, 139n2, 141n32, 144n70, 145n78; mode of writing of, 33–38, 59–60, 123, 137, 141n27; *Nicomachean Ethics*, xi, 2–6, 21, 25, 65, 72, 83, 139n5, 139n6, 140n10, 142n35, 142n42; *Physics*, 91; *Poetics*, xi, 34, 131; *Politics*, xi, 8, 30–31, 44, 61, 65–66, 85, 96–97, 101–2, 121–22, 137, 139n2
autonomy, 5, 95, 98. *See also* self-sufficiency
autotelic, 127, 134, 136

Barker, Sir Ernest, 65, 90
beautiful (the), 3, 6–7, 72, 122. *See also kalon*

cannibalism, 17–19, 24, 26–27, 139n4, 139n5
Carthage, 35–36, 42, 136
censorship, 136–37
chance, 92, 98–99, 102, 157

change, 6, 97, 99
children, 25, 35, 96
circle-men, 93–96, 110, 146n85
citizens, 47–48, 68, 78, 113–14; of the best regime, 124–25, 128; Hippodamus on, 37–38
city, 7, 46, 60, 85, 87; parts of, 75, 80, 127–28; as self-aware, 47, 61, 87; self-identity of, 45–40, 141n26. *See also polis*
class jumping, 22, 31, 101
communism, 40, 146n83
convention, 8–9, 16. *See also nomos*
courage, 3, 41, 83
Crete, 35–36, 41–42
crime, 87
cyclops, 17, 25, 147n101

democracy, 7, 10, 46–48, 50–52, 54, 56, 59, 67–68; 73–74, 77, 80–82, 84, 87, 89, 101–17, 139n2, 141n31, 142n36, 143n60, 144n74; *êthos* of, 106–8; institutions of, 106–8, 114–15; and oligarchy, 81–82, 115–16; varieties of, 112–13
dêmos, 47, 69, 82, 92, 103, 109, 127–28, 130, 144n74

education, 25, 131, 133–37, 139n2
epistêmê, 72. *See also* science
equality, 10, 23, 31, 69, 108, 122; as principle of justice, 55–57
erôs, 93–95, 145n79

149

About the Author

Michael Davis has taught philosophy at Sarah Lawrence College since 1977 and teaches political philosophy in the graduate program of the Political Science Department at Fordham University. He is the author of *Aristotle's* Poetics: *The Poetry of Philosophy* (Lanham, Maryland: Rowman & Littlefield, 1992) and *Ancient Tragedy and the Origins of Modern Science* (Carbondale: Southern Illinois University Press, 1988) as well as numerous essays on Plato, Aristotle, and Shakespeare. He is currently working on a book on Rousseau's *The Reveries of a Solitary Walker*.